D0860599

The Great Betrayal

Also by Nicholas Bethell

Gomulka: His Poland and His Communism
The War Hitler Won
The Last Secret
The Palestine Triangle

The Great Betrayal

The Untold Story of
Kim Philby's Biggest Coup

NICHOLAS BETHELL

HODDER AND STOUGHTON
LONDON SYDNEY AUCKLAND TORONTO

British Library Cataloguing in Publication Data
Bethell, Nicholas
The great betrayal.
1. Intelligence service—History—20th century
2. Albania—Politics and government—1944–
327.496′5 DR977

ISBN 0 340 35701 0

Copyright © 1984 by Nicholas Bethell. First printed 1984. All rights reserved. No part of this publication may be reproduced or transmitted in any form or by any means, electronic or mechanical, including photocopy, recording, or any information storage and retrieval system, without permission in writing from the publisher. *Printed in Great Britain for Hodder and Stoughton Limited, Mill Road, Dunton Green, Sevenoaks, Kent by St Edmundsbury Press, Bury St Edmunds, Suffolk. Typeset by Hewer Text Composition Services, Edinburgh.*

Hodder and Stoughton Editorial Office: 47 Bedford Square, London WC1B 3DP.

Contents

Acknowledgements

My thanks are primarily to Olwen Gillespie, who worked with me during the years I spent on this project, encouraged me to proceed and helped to provide the essential skeleton of documents on which the flesh of verbal testimony could properly hang.

Of the many Albanians who assisted I recall particularly Darvish Duma who introduced me to my initial contacts in the scattered communities, Mrs Kimete Basha who found and summarised the basic Albanian language books on the subject and Sali Toptani who translated for me the archives of the Legaliteti movement, the transcript of the Shehu/Matjani trial and other vital papers.

I wish to thank all those Albanians who took part in the operation and told me of their experiences. I thank them for the courage with which they endured the pain of such bitter recollection. I am grateful too, to the American and British participants who agreed to discuss the story with me. I appreciate that, after some reflection, they decided to trust me to handle this sensitive matter fairly and responsibly. I hope that I haven't disappointed them.

To those American and British participants who declined to discuss the affair, I would say only that I accept and respect their decision. All those who venture into public discussion of the maze of the secret world seek a nice balance between two contradictory considerations, the need to protect national security and the right of citizens to know what is done in their name. It is only to be expected that some will disagree with others on where the crucial line should be drawn. Finally, I would like to thank my housekeeper, Ana Pinho, for providing me with the conditions at home in which I could think about these complicated problems and assemble the book. I thank her for putting up with a writer's moodiness and doubts.

The photograph of Kim Philby is the copyright of Popperfoto.

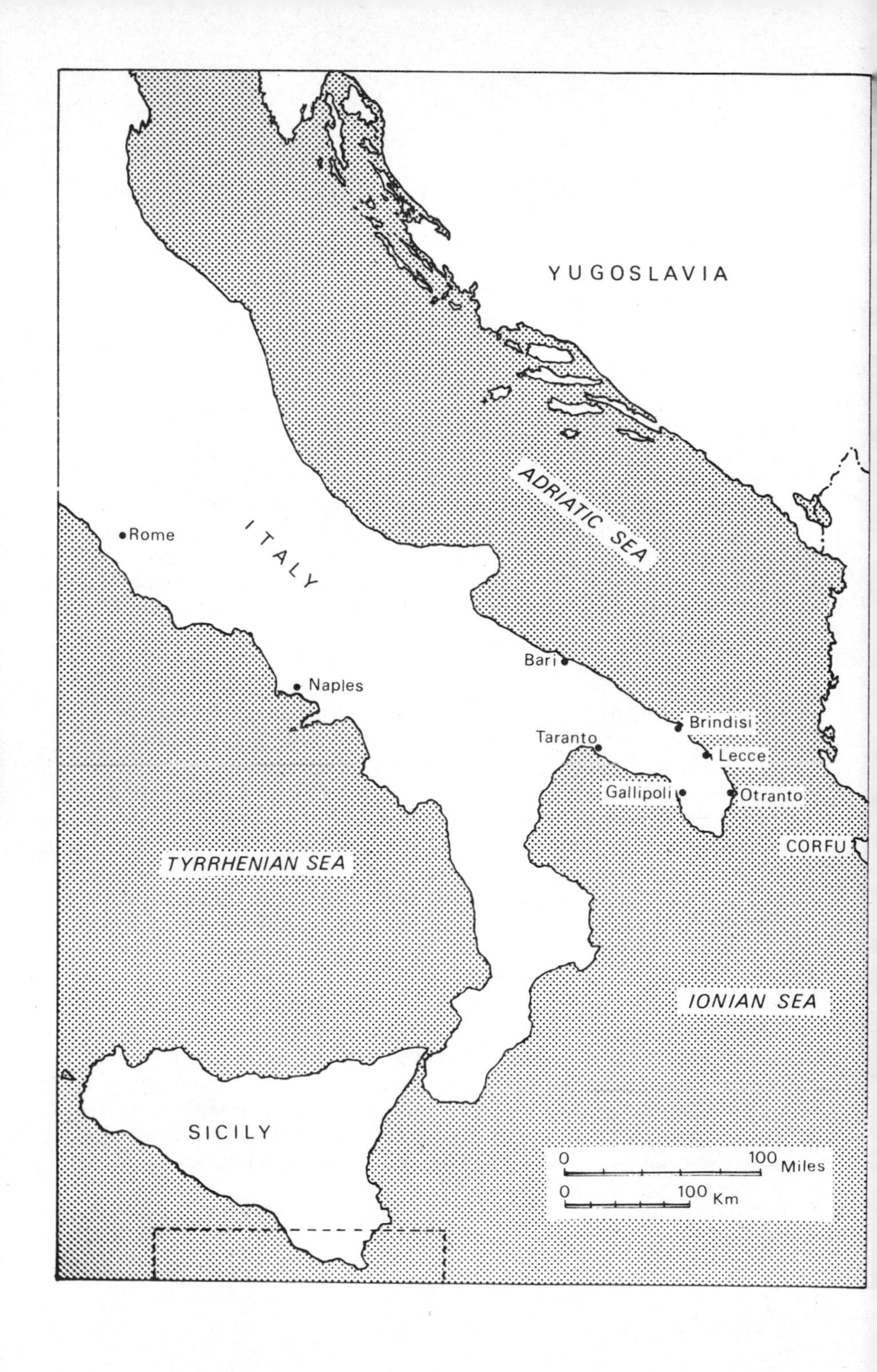

YUGOSLAVIA
ADRIATIC SEA
ITALY
Rome
Naples
Bari
Brindisi
Taranto
Lecce
Gallipoli
Otranto
CORFU
TYRRHENIAN SEA
IONIAN SEA
SICILY
0
100 Miles
0
100 Km

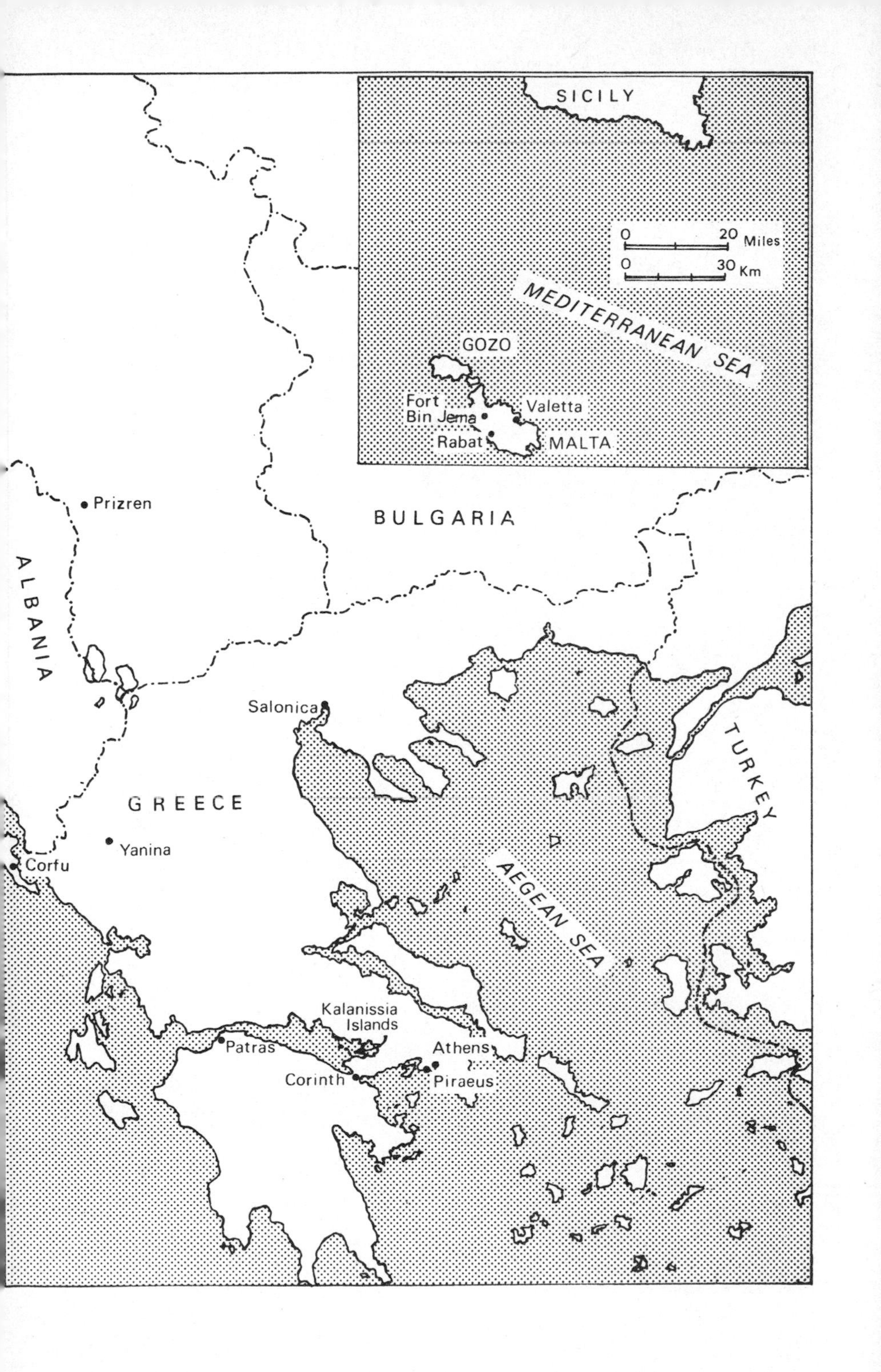
SICILY
0 20 Miles
0 30 Km
MEDITERRANEAN SEA
GOZO
Fort
Bin Jema
Valetta
Rabat
MALTA
Prizren
BULGARIA
ALBANIA
Salonica
TURKEY
GREECE
Yanina
Corfu
AEGEAN SEA
Kalanissia
Islands
Athens
Patras
Corinth
Piraeus

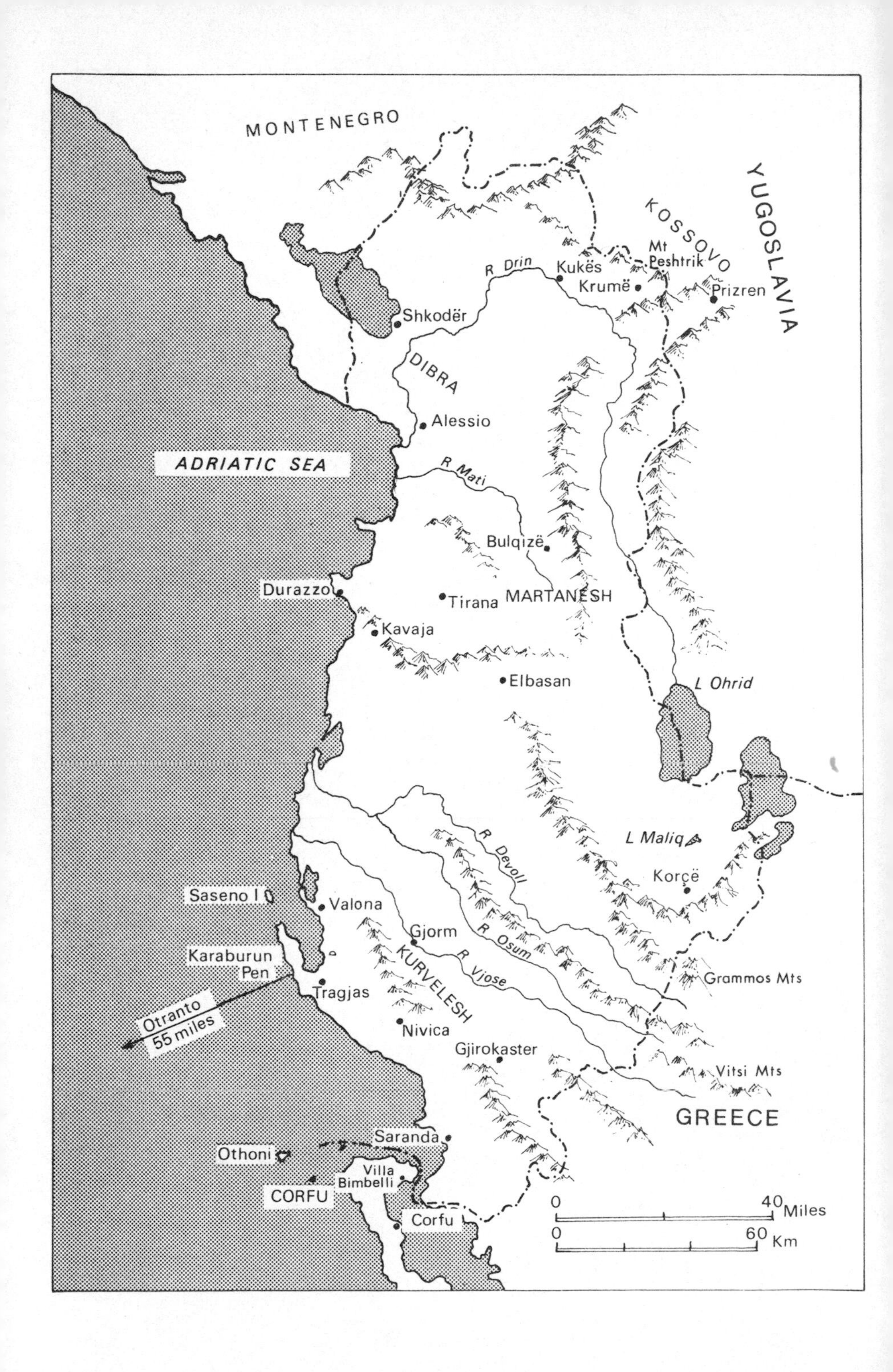
MONTENEGRO
YUGOSLAVIA
KOSSOVO
Mt Peshtrik
R Drin
Kukës
Krumë
Prizren
Shkodër
DIBRA
Alessio
ADRIATIC SEA
R Mati
Bulqizë
Durazzo
Tirana
MARTANESH
Kavaja
Elbasan
L Ohrid
L Maliq
R Devoll
Korçë
Saseno I
Valona
Gjorm
R Osum
Karaburun Pen
KURVELESH
R Vjose
Grammos Mts
Tragjas
Otranto 55 miles
Nivica
Gjirokaster
Vitsi Mts
GREECE
Saranda
Othoni
Villa Bimbelli
CORFU
Corfu
0
40
Miles
0
60
Km

Introduction

During the night of October 3rd/4th, 1949, two young Englishmen edged their boat towards Karaburun, a peninsula that sticks up out of the Albanian coastline and into the eastern Adriatic like the thumb of a half-open hand. They were Sam Barclay and John Leatham. Their boat was a forty-three-ton schooner, the *Stormie Seas*, so named because it put them in mind of the lines of an anonymous fifteenth-century poet:

> Rest after toyle, port
> After stormie seas,
> Death after life, these
> Things do greatlie please.

Painted blue and gold with four bright orange sails, she looked like a local Greek fishing vessel with the finish of a luxury cruiser, the sort that rich men charter to take their friends on eastern Mediterranean cruises. Sam's wife Eileen was on board and their dog, named 'Lean-to' after her. There was Dino Mavros,[1] their Greek boatman, and two other Englishmen known as Derby and Lofty. Anyone approaching them would have taken them for an English group enjoying their boating holiday.

The truth was rather different. Leatham and Barclay were not holiday sailors, but ex-naval officers who had served in the Aegean during the war and then run supplies from Athens to Salonika in their own boat, the *Bessie*, to help Greek government forces against communist rebels in the civil war that followed. In October 1948 they had been recruited by Pat Whinney, representing British intelligence in Athens, and they were now on a mission of subversion and sabotage against Enver Hoxha's communist Albanian government.

A closer look at the *Stormie Seas* would have revealed her true purpose. Her pretty sails were not her only source of power. She also had a huge engine, a ninety-horsepower Ruston-Hornsby, taking up the entire hold and giving her a respectable eight knots. And in the saloon below, Barclay's clever drawings concealed removable partitions behind which lay several secret compartments and dummy fuel tanks. It was here that they kept their radio equipment and code-books.

The most bizarre part of her cargo was, however, human – nine little men, known as 'pixies' by the British, all armed and in uniform, equipped with all the latest inventions in the repertoire of guerilla warfare. They had been trained by British experts in Malta precisely for this moment. They had two radio sets, since shortly after landing they were going to divide into two groups. Two men were assigned to carry each radio, one for the set itself, the other for the generator, a folding frame with pedals operated by a man who lay on his back and 'bicycled' the necessary electricity.

They were from Albania's southern region and, as several spoke Greek, Mavros was able to sit with them and try to talk them out of their nervousness. They took special pride in their new British army watches. These were a symbol of their new status as the vanguard in the West's new policy of retaliation against Stalin's aggressive moves. However, each watch was also a reminder of the dangers that would face them when they landed. A lethal cyanide pill was taped to the outside of the strap. It would take little more than a second for any man in a hopeless position to lower his head, bite off the tape and swallow the pill even with his hands tied in front of him.

At precisely this time there was another much more senior British agent also on the high seas, though in very different circumstances. He had left Southampton on October 1st on board the *Caronia*, a P and O liner, on his way to take up the position of Washington representative of the Secret Intelligence Service (SIS), also known as MI6. Until the summer of 1949 he had been the British embassy's 'passport officer' in Istanbul, but he had just been given a far more important assignment and he had spent a month in London being briefed about it. His name was Kim Philby.

He accepted the job, as he later wrote in his KGB-doctored memoirs, because it took him 'right back into the middle of intelligence policy making' and because it gave him 'a close-up view of the American intelligence organisations'.[2] These included the Federal Bureau of Investigation, which controls American internal security, and the Central Intelligence Agency, which gathers information overseas. He was also Britain's link-man with a now defunct body known as the Office for Policy Coordination (OPC), whose role it was to carry out sabotage and subversion in European countries unfriendly to the United States. They and SIS had looked at Stalin's satellite empire and selected Albania as their first target.

The nine Albanians on board the *Stormie Seas* had spent September 1949 completing their training in Malta under the command of Lieutenant-Colonel David Smiley, a man with a brilliant war record, much of it spent in Albania fighting the German occupying army. He taught them the techniques of Special Operations Executive (SOE), Britain's main anti-Nazi subversive body during the war years. They had agreed to put themselves under British protection and to use British sponsorship to overthrow the communist government, which they hated. They saw themselves not as British puppets, but as patriots using the British to free their homeland.

Philby had spent the same month in London being briefed about his exciting new assignment, the CIA and SIS having agreed to close collaboration over a wide range of issues. One of these was the Albanian operation. Philby was appointed as its joint 'commander' and it was to be part of his job to coordinate the operation's two sides with his American opposite number. In order to do this effectively, he needed to be informed of the preparatory work that had already been done and of the landing that was to take place early the following month.

Before the *Caronia* reached New York on October 8th Philby spent an enjoyable voyage, as he records, drinking the case of champagne delivered to his cabin by a 'disgustingly rich' friend and talking to the cartoonist Osbert Lancaster who happened to be making the same journey. He took up his post two days later in Washington under the cover of first secretary at the embassy. By then the young Albanians had spent a week back in their own country, picking their way through the hills towards the region where they had friends and family. It was wild, deserted countryside and there seemed little danger that they would run into a government patrol.

They did not know it, but their mission had already been betrayed. Philby had seen to that. He was a double agent committed for many years to serving Stalin's secret service rather than that of his own country. He met one of his Soviet contacts in September before leaving London, as he writes, and there can be no doubt that he told him about the Albanian affair, including the short-term plans for a landing in Karaburun. It cannot have taken long for this timely piece of information to reach Moscow headquarters and to be sent on to Tirana, the Albanian capital. The Sigurimi, the local secret police, had been trained by their Soviet colleagues to deal with such emergencies.

Underground movements live on the basis of tight security and mutual trust. They cannot survive, let alone operate, if their instructions are consistently made known to the authorities of the regime they are trying to subvert. Philby's existence as a traitor in the very centre of American-British intelligence cooperation is therefore reason enough, even though there were other reasons too, why the Albanian venture was fated to fail.

Hardly anyone knows that the United States and Britain chose to make Albania, Europe's poorest country, a secret battleground between West and East, the central point of their efforts to regain the initiative in the Cold War that began the previous year in 1948. Stalin had taken a number of aggressive steps. He engineered a communist takeover in Czechoslovakia, then blockaded Berlin, forcing the United States to supply the city by air at enormous cost, and he stepped up his encouragement and assistance to communist rebels trying to overthrow the Greek government by force. By the end of 1948 the West was determined to retaliate.

The Albanian affair was conceived by American and British officials at a meeting in Washington, then approved by government leaders. It was a carefully considered act of policy based on the idea that Stalin would be impressed by a Western decision to act against him militarily, even on a small scale and in an outpost of his empire. It would make him think twice before launching further aggressive enterprises. It might also, incidentally, detach Albania from the Soviet orbit, ending Enver Hoxha's harsh rule and allowing the emergence of a kinder and less anti-Western government.

The military side began in October 1949 when the first teams of armed British-trained agents were landed on Albanian territory. It ended in the last days of 1953 when the failure of an important American-sponsored mission was publicly revealed. Agents were captured and put on trial. All this was proclaimed by Albanian newspapers and radio. The Soviet media referred to it from time to time, but whereas they gave massive coverage to the trials of 'spies' and 'traitors' nearer home, to the point of paranoia, since most of them were quite innocent, they minimised the genuine Western intelligence and subversion enterprise in Albania.

No one in the West noticed the Albanian government's complaints. Or, if they did, they dismissed them as the typical outpourings of a dictatorship crazed with spy-mania. Neither Congress nor Parliament questioned their administrations about the secret war being waged. They simply knew nothing about it. In fact, hardly a soul outside the intelligence world and the government elite was told that it even existed. And this remained so for more than a decade.

In the late 1960s, after the enormity of Philby's treachery was revealed, teams of specialist writers and investigators began examining his career, among them three staff members of the *Sunday Times* in London. Their book, published in 1968, revealed the operation's existence and Philby's key role in it as joint commander. Since then various other books on the secret world have touched on the episode, but never in any detail. This is because the two governments involved still cover it with a blanket of secrecy and try to prevent its facts from being researched.

Not only do they decline to reveal operational details or names of agents involved – this would be understandable – but they also will not even admit that it happened. They will not deny that it happened either. They maintain this silence more than thirty years after the last big parachute landing in May 1953 and in spite of the evidence of more than a hundred people – British, American and Albanian – who took part in the attempt and have described what they did, believing that the public interest is best served by the truth.

The records of British intelligence in peacetime are never made public, so it is no surprise if the papers describing this particular episode are not available either. British people who took part in it are still, strictly speaking, bound by the all-embracing Official Secrets Act not to discuss it. It is, however, assumed that the Act would not be enforced over events so long past. Some have asked the British authorities how they should respond to inquiries made by the author of this book. The replies they receive are not as restrictive as one might expect. They have been told to bear in mind their responsibilities to protect national security and the safety of individuals, but otherwise to use their own judgement.

The United States's attitude to the release of official information is usually more liberal than Britain's. There is, after all, the Freedom of Information Act. One might think that such an enlightened law would allow something at least to be made public about what took place thirty-five years ago. However, the American attitude is even more secretive than the British. The United States insists on maintaining its 'capacity for plausible denial' over the Albanian operation, even though the denial now seems no longer plausible. Its government has ordered, under threat of prosecution, all those involved to say nothing whatever about their part in the operation, not even to admit that there was an operation at all. The CIA reminds them of their obligations by sending them copies of secrecy undertakings signed during the 1940s. Several of the Americans mentioned in this book have received such warnings.

In September 1982 Louis J. Dube, information review officer for the CIA's Directorate of Operations, declared under oath: 'Plaintiff's FOIA request which seeks information on alleged attempts to conduct covert Agency intelligence operations in Albania between 1945 and 1953 can neither be confirmed nor denied, as an affirmative or negative answer to plaintiff's FOIA request could reasonably be expected to cause serious damage to the national security.'

Dube's affidavit explains that any statement on the Albanian affair could damage present or future relations with the Albanian government, that it would aid the Soviet Union by confirming or denying what Philby told them about it. Until that happens, according to the CIA, the Soviet Union 'cannot know the accuracy of what was passed to them by Kim Philby'. Any CIA answer to the FOIA request 'would resolve this mystery' for them. And this would be damaging.

The idea that Philby has for decades been lying to Soviet intelligence about his participation in the Albanian operation seems very improbable, so much so that one looks for other reasons to explain CIA's determination to hide this small piece of history. Are they embarrassed to admit that they trained armed men and sent them into a foreign country in time of peace? Are they worried by the thought that they failed? Maybe so, but one does not find the same coyness in the American attitude to other secret ventures of long ago.

Why then do they persist? Why will they not now, decades after the event, allow the people to know what they did and to learn from their mistakes? The answer to the riddle will emerge in the pages that follow.

1 Why Albania?

Albania is in most western minds a country as unreal as Ruritania or Transylvania. Why then should the West have made it their unknown arena for a tiny experimental hot war? Part of the answer lies in Albania's alarming background of outlandish history, harsh geography and almost continual civil strife. All of this is fundamental to any understanding of the origins of the 1949 conspiracy.

Isolated from the rest of the world, always under foreign attack or occupation, the Albanian people early in their history formed the notion that outsiders are murderous enemies, that family or local ties are the only valid basis of trust. Strangers found no way of building friendships with Albanians or travelling through its valleys in safety. Those few that ventured in noticed only the lawless nature of the inhabitants, the backwardness of their civilisation and the obscurity of their language. The foreigner is in Albanian eyes a threat or a spy, or at best a lost explorer who cannot work out who these people are.

It is a rough rectangle, 120 miles by 40 miles stood up at one end, squashed between Greece and Yugoslavia facing the eastern Adriatic and Italy's heel. Its population is put officially at 2.7 million. There are 200,000 living in its capital, Tirana, and no more than 70,000 in any other town. The land is so mountainous that only one-third can be effectively cultivated. Its communist system is the purest and harshest of them all. No Albanian may own a private car or go abroad for a holiday. It is a serious criminal offence to practise any religion.

The Illyrian tribes who were the Albanians' forefathers were first invaded by Rome's legions, who built a military road from Durazzo (Durrës) through Macedonia to Constantinople. About 700AD Slav tribes swept south across the River Danube wreaking havoc along the eastern Adriatic and driving people into the hills. In the eleventh century Byzantium was the dominating force in the area and in the early fourteenth century it was Stephen Dushan's Serbian empire. In 1385 armies of the Ottoman empire reached the Albanian coast and within a few years the local people were paying Turkish taxes.

Five centuries of Ottoman subjection were illuminated at the outset by the flash of George Kastrioti's rebellion. Skanderbeg, as he was known, served in the Turkish army before returning to his native soil around 1430 and leading his people against their oppressors, reconverting many of them to Christianity. A skilful politician and military commander, he persuaded local chiefs to join him in twenty-five years of successful resistance, removing the occupiers and punishing the punitive expeditions sent against him, before withdrawing from the fray and dying of natural causes in 1468. He is Albania's best-known figure and their national hero. There is a poem about him by Longfellow and an opera by Vivaldi.

Albanians became distinguished servants of the Ottoman empire and several achieved the position of Grand Vizier. The most famous was Mohammed Ali, Viceroy of Egypt from 1805 to 1848, who made Egypt semi-independent of Istanbul and founded the royal dynasty that ruled Egypt until King Farouk's departure in 1952. It was possible for Albanians, as for other Ottoman subjects, to better themselves by learning Turkish and adopting Turkish ways, though at the cost of depriving the country of its culture, national identity and most talented sons. During the nineteenth century a few Austrian and Italian schools were built, lessening the nation's dependence on Turkey but doing little to advance the national idea. The Albanian language was suppressed by the Turks to prevent its becoming a rallying point.

In the first years of the twentieth century Ottoman rule began to crumble and the revolution of the Young Turks allowed a national Albanian congress to meet in 1909, with a plan for local autonomy within the empire. In 1912 a national uprising induced the Young Turks to grant independence. All Europe was searched for possible kings and various candidates, however unlikely, were put forward, including the English cricketer C. B. Fry. The choice eventually fell on a German prince. Then in 1914 the Balkans disintegrated into war and the fledgling Albanian nation was one of the first casualties. Greece occupied the south, Italy took Valona and Serbia briefly took the north before being supplanted by Austro-Hungary. Ever since then Albanians have been obsessed by the fear that Greeks, Yugoslavs and Italians covet their territory.

After the war Italy and Greece seemed determined to press their claim, but at Versailles President Woodrow Wilson persuaded the victorious powers to make Albania an independent state. In 1920 the skeleton of a government was put together in Tirana with Ahmet Zogu as minister of the interior. But it was a land without laws or institutions, a people without education or the means to acquire it, a valley society without the means of communication needed to enforce the writ of central government.

Ahmet Zogu, the key to Albanian politics from 1920 onwards, was the son of a central Albanian highland chief whose father had plotted against the Sultan, as a result of which Ahmet was taken as a hostage to the imperial court to guarantee the father's good behaviour. He became a colonel in the Ottoman army at a young age and was set to follow the path of other Albanians up the ladder of Turkish imperial power when Albania became independent and he returned home. When the Austro-Hungarians threw the Serbs out of the north, he joined their army and again reached the rank of colonel, then served as an aide to the Emperor Franz Joseph in Vienna.

When the war ended he was twenty-three years old, with two military careers behind him and much wisdom and experience gleaned from service at the heart of two imperial courts, the Ottoman and the Habsburg. In 1922, at the age of twenty-seven, he became Albania's prime minister. Thereafter, apart from a brief period in 1924 when he was forced to take refuge in Yugoslavia, he governed the country continuously. He became president in February 1925 and was proclaimed King Zog I in September 1928.

He could not give his country complete independence. Albania had a population of only one million, almost all of them peasants farming poor land. So he turned to Mussolini's Italy and during 1925–6 signed two agreements granting Italy political privilege in return for financial support. His government was authoritarian. The British politician Julian Amery, who knew King Zog and describes him as the most impressive man he ever met, calls it 'a wonderfully liberal dictatorship'. It was his achievement to have kept Albania stable and semi-independent for nearly two decades.

King Zog of Albania is dimly recalled by many in the outside world as the mythical figure who ruled a legendary country. Although criticised for his lavish lifestyle and the extravagance of his six sisters, which contrasted ill with the poverty of his subjects, he brought considerable colour and a dash of romance to the new nation. Rumour has it, for instance, that while on a state visit to Austria he was waylaid by an assassin in the foyer of the Vienna opera house. He did not run or hide from the man who fired at him. Instead he drew his own pistol and shot the man dead.

Proceeding to Budapest, it is said, he was driving down a street in an open carriage when he saw a beautiful young woman walking along the pavement. 'Stop the carriage,' he shouted. He spoke to the girl and immediately fell in love with her. She was Countess Geraldine Apponyi, the daughter of a poor but noble Hungarian family. He took her home to Tirana and married her.

Their son Leka was born in April 1939, a few days after Hitler's forces occupied Prague. It was the signal for Mussolini to show that he too could seize European land. Albania was easy pickings. On April 18th the King and Queen fled with their three-day-old son to Greece and their country became an Italian province. The British government, obsessed by the need to appease the two dictators, did not protest. And when the King came to Britain after France's defeat in 1940, it was as a refugee, not as head of a government-in-exile. He and Queen Geraldine took a house near Henley-on-Thames near Oxford, while his sisters stayed at London's Savoy hotel.

Albania was left to the Italians, though by 1941 it was possible to detect the beginnings of a resistance movement. Abas Kupi, a famous fighter and the King's greatest supporter, returned home and started rallying men to restore the monarchy. His party, known as Legaliteti, was based on a legal interpretation of the King's royal prerogatives. He had not abdicated and had left Albania while still in possession of the people's and Parliament's mandate. It is a position that Zog was always to maintain. And his son maintains it today.

At the same time a communist movement began to appear after Hitler's invasion of Russia in June 1941. Its leaders were mainly intellectuals who had fled Zog's rule and spent the 1930s in western Europe. They quickly came under the influence of the much larger communist movement in Yugoslavia, led by Josip Broz Tito, and it was with the help of two Yugoslav envoys that the Albanians in November 1941 gave birth to a communist party, electing as secretary-general Enver Hoxha, a schoolteacher from Korçë and former student of Montpellier university in France. It was a position that Hoxha was to retain for more than forty years.

The third resistance group, known as Balli Kombëtar (National Front), was led by such figures as Midhat Frasheri, a former diplomat and owner of Tirana's largest bookshop, and Abas Ermenji, also a native of Korçë and a French scholar. It was a social-democratic party, liberal, pro-Western and anti-royalist. The three groups were therefore as opposed to one another as they were to the foreign occupiers and their concern from 1941 to 1945 was as much about winning power after the war as about fighting Italians or Germans. Still, in the first two years they did operate against the occupying forces on a small scale without fratricidal strife.

The first two British agents, David Smiley and Neil (Billy) McLean, walked into Albania from Greece in April 1943 with little more than a submachine-gun each, a bag of gold and a wireless operator. They were received, not surprisingly, with caution. Eventually they found Enver Hoxha's partisan headquarters where they established their bona fides by successfully radioing for a parachute drop of arms, ammunition and gold sovereigns. The resistance leaders then realised that their strange uninvited guests could be valuable to them and took pains to cultivate the friendship.

This first mission to the partisans lasted six months. Smiley trained them, including their commander Mehmet Shehu, in the use of British weapons, explained the Western allies' tactics, lived, ate and joked with them. On one occasion Enver Hoxha gave him, using a map with every country marked in red, a lecture on how the new communist order was going to be established across the globe. Smiley, a believer in Britain's imperial mission, answered, 'I'd like to see the world painted red all over too, but not the red you're thinking about.'

Their relationship was good-natured, but their mutual suspicions never far below the surface. Hoxha saw the British as little better than spies and fascist collaborators: 'I put a tight rein on their desires, which were simply to gather information and carry out espionage . . . They wanted to gather information about everything, to learn our strength, tactics and strategy.'[3] McLean and Smiley felt that the partisans had no wish to fight the enemy, that their aim was merely to exploit British prestige and equipment against the non-communist groups.

Smiley became irritated by the partisans' crude attempts to exaggerate their exploits. If they fired a few shots at an enemy convoy, they would claim that they had ambushed it and killed large numbers. He remembers an occasion when the Italian army attacked a partisan position and Shehu's men simply ran away: 'At the time I thought it was cowardice, but then I realised that these were their orders, not to engage the enemy unless absolutely necessary, to fire a few shots from time to time to impress British officers, to accept all the arms that the stupid British dropped them and keep them for the civil war.'

Smiley, McLean and Julian Amery were the three key figures of British involvement in Albania. Young men in their early twenties, they were members of the elite Special Operations Executive (SOE) that carried out sabotage and gathered information behind enemy lines. Smiley was the younger son of a baronet, no politician but a brilliant soldier, an expert at making explosions and dealing with an enemy at close range. McLean was a professional soldier too, a Sandhurst graduate and a man of keen intellect, a Scottish highlander brought up on a history of hill fighting and valley living.

Amery was the negotiator of the team, someone who looked at war and political struggle with something of the detachment of a chess player, who saw it as 'the big game'. He was the son of Leo Amery, secretary of state for India and one of Winston Churchill's closest friends. All were highly decorated for bravery in action, in addition to which they all developed an affection for Albanian people and an interest in their nation's future.

They and Alan Hare, another clever Etonian and the younger son of Lord Listowel, became the 'four musketeers' of the Albanian struggle, young men of influential family and with friends in high office. They had access to important ministers, including foreign secretary Anthony Eden and Harold Macmillan, minister resident in North-West Africa. And they did not share the general British wartime reverence of Stalin and the great Soviet ally. It was their duty, they felt, not only to fight Hitler's Germany, but also to oppose the spread of the communist doctrine with which they expected to find themselves in conflict as soon as the war was won.

It was not a fashionable position. In early 1943 the Red Army destroyed an entire German army group in Stalingrad, killing or capturing 350,000 of the enemy. Most British and American people saw Stalin as a hero and this was the prevailing mood at their base, SOE headquarters in Cairo, that communists were bearing the brunt of the war against Hitler, both in battle and in the underground resistance. It seemed to many, not only of left-wing persuasion, that communism was for many European countries the way of the future, that communist resistance movements were the most effective and that Britain should therefore give them the bulk of her support.

Some of the SOE officers, like the writer James Klugman, were communist party members. Others like Basil Davidson, James Eyre and Reg Hibbert were men of the political left and opposed to the line taken by McLean and Amery. McLean says of Elliot Watrous, who succeeded Philip Leake as head of the Albanian section, 'He had very "progressive" views and we felt that he was supporting the communist cause against the nationalists at every level.' It was left to the 'musketeers' and a handful of others – Tony Neel, John Hibberdine, Anthony Northrop, Peter Kemp and Tony Simcox – to form an anti-Stalinist minority in the Balkan section of SOE, for which they found themselves labelled by the rest as 'the fascist spies'.

Hoxha's own colourful memoirs outline his version of McLean in some detail: 'He smiled as he squeezed my hand. He laughed, his eyes gleamed like those of a fox. He was intelligent, but he had a black heart.' This was during the summer of 1943 when the two British officers lived with the communists, trained with them and supplied them with weapons, mortars and anti-tank rifles, hardware that they would never have obtained elsewhere, and substantial amounts of money, gold sovereigns dropped from the sky in little heavy bags of a thousand coins each. Money was an important weapon of war, especially in the Balkans where it could buy not only weapons and mules, but also the allegiance of waverers.

By the end of the summer the First Partisan Brigade commanded by Hoxha's lieutenant Mehmet Shehu was 500 strong and quite well equipped. But conditions in the country were very hard and people were starving. Orders came for McLean and Smiley to be evacuated and they made for the coast, a rocky inlet on the Karaburun peninsula south of Valona, a spot they called 'Seaview'. Their supplies ran out and they spent their last ten days living on a dead mule and water that they sucked out of the rocks with a sponge.

One night in October 1943 a motor torpedo boat finally arrived from across the straits. It got close inshore and British sailors threw crates of food on to the rocks for the benefit of the hungry Albanians. Then the two British officers made for the boat in a rubber dinghy that leaked, with Smiley rowing and McLean bailing, until it sank ten yards from the boat. Each used one arm to swim the final stretch, with the other arm holding their briefcases full of secret papers out of the water, until they were close enough for the sailors to reach out and haul them on board.

In July 1943 the Allies had landed in Sicily and a few days later Mussolini's government fell. His successor Marshal Badoglio made peace with the Allies in September, declaring war on Germany the following month. Albania, it seemed for a moment, was on the point of liberation as 20,000 leaderless Italian soldiers roamed the country looking for food and resistance groups took control of the towns and villages without a struggle. Germany reacted quickly, however, sending a crack parachute division into Tirana that chased the disunited guerillas out of towns and villages.

The 1943–4 winter was crucial to Albania's civil struggle. German forces moved into the country from Yugoslavia and exacted a fearful revenge for the humiliations endured by the troops of Hitler's ally. They invaded villages, hounded the resistance, burnt, looted and killed. The fighters usually escaped, but the civilians were left destitute, with nothing but their wives and children. Reg Hibbert, who was parachuted into the northern highlands in December 1943, recalls being constantly on the move, trying to feel out the ground, make contacts and gauge who was effective. At that stage, he concluded, with every Albanian struggling to stay alive, resistance was insignificant.

The difference between the groups was that, whereas the royalists and Balli Kombëtar wanted to preserve Albania's traditional structures, the partisans wanted to destroy them. They did not care if the Germans destroyed property and killed livestock. On the contrary, it helped their cause. Hibbert says, 'Villagers' homes were being burnt in wintertime. What were they to do? If they stayed behind, they were slaughtered or they froze or they starved. So they fled from the villages into the hills with their children, which was all they had. And who was there to receive them? The ragged partisans.'

It was a vicious circle that suited British and American interests, at least in the short term. Ihsan Toptani, a rich Albanian with many influential friends, points out that the complications of war had left Britain with little concern for the future of Albania, one of Hitler's smallest victims: 'They were just interested in Churchill's order to kill as many Germans as possible. We said, "We have nothing against that, but at the same time we don't want to destroy ourselves for the sake of a slogan. We don't want to kill two Germans and have three Albanian villages razed to the ground in reprisal."'

It is one of the few things that Amery and Hibbert agree on, that the nationalists fought the Germans less than the partisans, not because they were pro-German, but because they represented pre-occupation vested interests, whereas Hoxha represented the dispossessed and was uninhibited about the destruction that his activities caused. A British report of 1943 judged that 'so far the partisans have proved the better fighters and the Balli the finer gentlemen'.[4]

Amery believes that Britain should have understood the nationalists' hesitation and taken a broader view of British interest than a simple order to 'kill Germans'. 'It is arguable that the communist partisans were the better fighters,' he says. 'When we were losing the war, my own strong recommendation was to support the communists. But by the middle of 1943, after El Alamein and Stalingrad, it was pretty clear that we would win the war. What mattered then was who would take power in occupied countries after the Germans withdrew.'

In early December 1943, on his return from the Teheran conference with Roosevelt and Stalin, Churchill indicated at a dinner attended by Amery that he would back the royalists in Greece, the communists in Yugoslavia. And by the end of the year he had indeed acted along these lines, abandoning Mihailović in favour of Tito. But Albania, it seems, was not mentioned at the Teheran meeting and was not put before the three leaders as a political problem. Yugoslav advisers were appearing in greater numbers among Hoxha's groups and already Albania was being treated by the three powers like a provincial offshoot, not important enough for the Big Three even to think about. The 'musketeers'' warnings about communist influence in Albania seemed very unimportant.

The Germans hoped to eliminate resistance during the winter months, when life in the hills is very hard. They killed many, but not enough to destroy Shehu's brigade, which was the nucleus. And when spring came the partisans found themselves with thousands of new recruits driven to join them by the harshness of the German methods. They then began to fight, not as much as they claimed, but enough to establish their credentials with British officers who, especially after Churchill's order on Yugoslavia, were already inclined to favour the communist side. And, as the partisans stepped up their armed resistance, the Germans increased their reprisals, driving more men from the villages to the partisan bands and intensifying the vicious circle.

By the time McLean and Smiley parachuted back into Albania with Amery in April 1944, the balance had moved strongly in the communists' favour. The traditional leaders had lost not only their property, but also their authority. Unable to inspire their people to rebellion or to protect them from German reaction to Shehu's assaults, they lost face not only with the Albanians, but also with the British in Cairo. SOE did not think about what was to happen after the war and they took the simple view that the partisans were doing more fighting and killing more Germans, so they deserved to get the British supplies of arms and money.

Hoxha's attitude to Britain became more and more defiant. Anthony Northrop, who was attached to his headquarters, remembers setting up a coordinated attack on a German position in early 1944. A time was agreed when the partisans would attack it and the Royal Air Force would bomb it from Italy. At the last moment Hoxha called off his part of the attack. Northrop was angry and immediately radioed SOE headquarters in Bari in southern Italy to cancel all supply drops to the communists. Hoxha reacted by taking away Northrop's radio and confining him to a house under guard.

A little later, after things were smoothed over, Northrop was woken up before dawn one morning by an Albanian who said there were Germans on their way to search the village. He asked the villager, where were the others? Where were the partisans from headquarters who had bedded down with him a few hours before? It emerged that Hoxha and his men had already crept away, having been warned about the German patrol some time earlier. Northrop says, 'I never felt quite the same about Hoxha after that. I got out of the house just a couple of minutes ahead of the German soldiers. I took a very dim view of Hoxha simply going off and leaving me behind.'

SOE headquarters were again told about Hoxha's unfriendly acts, but still they kept supporting him. This is the core of the argument that still rages among those British officers who took part in the Albanian war.

Why did SOE headquarters reject Britain's natural allies and support a communist movement? Would it have made a difference if they had supplied the royalists and Ballists instead? Would this have changed the outcome of the Albanian civil war? McLean, Smiley and Amery believe strongly that it would, that Britain made a mistake in not realising early enough that communism was the adversary of the future. The anti-communist resistance, they say, if it had been backed with British equipment and prestige, would at once have gained the motivation to fight and the confidence of the population.

Hibbert, Davidson and Watrous believe the opposite. They claim that German brutality was the communist side's recruiting officer and that no British action could have prevented the communist victory. In any case, they say, Tito was the strongest on-the-spot military force and he would never have permitted an anti-communist group to triumph in a country on his border that he proposed to control. It would therefore have been very dangerous to supply any side but the one that was fighting the occupying forces. McLean, Smiley and Amery were fighting the wrong enemy. Their activity was counter-productive in terms of the war effort and their advice was rightly rejected by SOE headquarters.

Amery describes these events vividly in his book *Sons of the Eagle*, how he and the nationalists, led by the royalist Kupi and the republican Ermenji, argued over whose duty it was to act first, he by arranging parachute drops or they by fighting the German garrisons. In August 1944 the nationalists began to act seriously in the north. Amery and McLean reported this to SOE headquarters, which had moved to Bari from Cairo, but still British supplies failed to arrive. 'This was the double-cross,' says Smiley. 'Kupi was promised air drops once he started fighting, but the drops never came. The Bari people had made up their minds that the partisans were the only people worth supporting.'

By the autumn of 1944 German forces were pulling out and the communists had won the civil war, but in Amery's view the game was still not lost: 'I was in Albania at that critical moment. With a very small British or American intervention we could have saved Albania for the West. This is what we did in Greece, after all. British forces stamped down on the communist resistance, bringing up General Zervas and the traditionalists.'

Amery disagrees with those who, echoing Churchill's remarks about Yugoslavia, feel that the West had no conceivable interest in Albania's future, let alone the right to influence it. There were two justifications, he says, one moral and one practical. Firstly, it was wrong to abandon the Albanians to Hoxha's evil regime and Stalin's imperial designs. Secondly, Valona and Saseno Island control the Strait of Otranto, the entrance to the Adriatic, an important naval gateway.

This was not the way the War Office saw the problem. On October 2nd they sent Bari an order on future policy:

> It does not seem therefore that it is within our power to prevent the emergence of a [partisan] government in Albania after the war. Owing to political views of partisan leaders it will look to Russia rather than to this country for support . . . We must therefore aim at strengthening our position with partisans now in order that after the war we may be able to influence the partisan government.[5]

Instead of moving in to overthrow the communists, as Amery wished, Britain proceeded to ingratiate herself with them. The British officers attached to non-communist groups were ordered by Bari to withdraw from the country. At the same moment Hoxha decided that he was strong enough now to dispense with British goodwill and assistance. He no longer had to treat courteously British agents who, he suspected, were spying on him and trying to corrupt his followers.

Tony Simcox, the officer accredited to Said Kryeziu and his brother Gani, leaders of Albanian guerillas from Kossovo in southern Yugoslavia, agreed with Amery's approach. He reported to Bari:

> We have let the nationalists of Albania down – especially Gani Kryeziu, who had fought well and is sacrificing more than any communist – by not being firmer with the FNC [partisans] when they attacked Kupi. We should have stopped, at once, all supplies and refused negotiations until they were prepared to fight only Germans. Allowing the communists to kill, attack or provoke their political enemies with our supplies is as bad as doing it ourselves.[6]

The partisans chose Simcox as their first victim. They surrounded his mission and, before taking him to their headquarters as a prisoner, they pulled down his tent, looted his kit, searched his papers and beat his interpreter to death.[7]

In the light of this event, McLean and Smiley were shocked to find themselves ordered by Bari to surrender to the communists for evacuation. It was done, Amery writes, to please Enver Hoxha, to prove that Britain was following his wishes by closing non-communist missions. McLean and Smiley did not, however, want to trust themselves to Hoxha's men or to dishonour their friend Abas Kupi by transferring themselves to his enemies' camp. Finally their dilemma was solved when Bari learnt that Hoxha intended to march McLean and Smiley south, to humiliate them as a demonstration of his own strength.[8] This was too much, even for Bari, who thereupon ordered the whole mission's evacuation by sea.

It was their duty, the three officers felt, to take Abas Kupi with them. 'In the kaleidoscope of politics all alliances and relationships are subject to the eternal laws of change,' writes Amery. Interests converge and separate, especially in war. And, since in the anarchy of international affairs necessity is the only law, it can be legitimate to abandon a cause or dissolve a pledge. It is always wrong, though, to abandon a faithful ally physically: 'We may have to jettison their interest and abjure support of their movements, but, if we cannot fulfil their hopes, we should leave no stone unturned to save at least their lives.'[9]

It was therefore, in Amery's view, 'to their eternal dishonour' that SOE headquarters decided not to evacuate Abas Kupi, fearing that this might impair their relations with Hoxha's communist partisans. This decision symbolises the view held by McLean, Smiley and other anti-communists who took part in the Albanian wartime resistance that SOE betrayed British interests and allies in pursuit of an objective – friendship after the war with Stalin and his followers – that was no more than a mirage.

Hibbert says, 'I am totally unmoved by Amery's outburst about Abas Kupi. We could all have played that game. Every mission had people to whom it was under some personal obligation. Kupi had no right to any special claim.' Smiley's reply is that Kupi's contribution was exceptional: 'Kupi lent us money when we ran out, money for food and mules, to keep us going. His men saved the lives of allied airmen, including Americans, who baled out after bomb runs over Rumania. He was promised supply drops if he fought and he was let down over that. And then he was abandoned to his fate. Hibbert's remarks are revolting.'

At the end of October 1944 two boats went from Bari to northern Albania and evacuated the 'musketeers', together with helpers. Their final indignity was to find that a British security officer had been sent by Bari with the rescue party specifically to make sure that no Albanian was taken on board. They reached Italy and at once sent angry telegrams to every influential figure they knew. The protests were effective and preparations for a mission to retrieve Kupi were in hand, but a few days later he arrived under his own steam, with his son Petrit and Ihsan Toptani, in a boat that he had himself obtained.

The three officers were debriefed and, as experienced agents, quickly sent to fight the other enemy in the Far East – Smiley to Thailand, Amery to China and McLean to Ceylon. The war was over in a few months and they returned home to more normal existence. Years passed, but still they seethed with anger at the way their cause in Albania had been mishandled, or even betrayed, and at the shameful way SOE headquarters had treated their comrades-in-arms. And Amery remembered his last meeting with Kupi, a game of chess that ended a few minutes before he left for the boat in the Mati estuary. Kupi, the illiterate tribesman, checkmated Amery's king, tapped the board and remarked that, God willing, the next round of the game would be played in Italy.

2 The need to retaliate

Enver Hoxha's provisional government set itself up in Tirana in November 1944 and proceeded to fulfil its opponents' worst expectations. People's courts presided over by untrained judges and egged on by bloodthirsty audience participation dealt out death sentences by the hundred to 'war criminals', a term which in practice included anyone advocating a non-communist viewpoint. In August 1945 a land reform decree abolished private estates, although by then most landowners had either been shot or had fled abroad. Religious activity was curtailed. On December 2nd, 1945, bogus elections were held without opposition candidates and a national assembly elected consisting entirely of communist supporters.

A United States mission under Joseph E. Jacobs and a British mission under Brigadier D. E. P. Hodgson preserved a token Western presence. In November 1945, on being assured that the forthcoming elections would be free, they provisionally recognised Hoxha's government. However, the conduct of the elections and the arrest in January 1946 of two men who had tried vainly to field opposition candidates, Gjergj Kokoshi and Suad Aslani, quickly demonstrated that this act of trust was premature. American and British representatives found themselves virtual prisoners in Tirana, unable to move about the country without a special pass and an escort provided for their 'protection'. Their employees were harassed by police.

On January 30th Hodgson reported that, as every Albanian knew, Gjergj Kokoshi's and Suad Aslani's only offence was to try and form an anti-communist political party. People were now waiting to see whether or not Britain and the United States did anything to protect them. On February 11th Hodgson wrote of 'a miniature reign of terror' against Catholics, non-communists, merchants and foreigners. On February 12th secretary of state James Byrnes protested about the Albanian government's 'disagreeable attitude', in particular their treatment of Jacobs and the deportation of his subordinates. On April 12th Jacobs reported persecution of the Greek minority.

In early May 1946 agreement was reached for a British legation to open in Tirana in place of the military mission, but it came to nothing when on May 15th two British cruisers, *Orion* and *Superb*, were fired on by Albanian guns from Saranda while sailing through the three-mile-wide Corfu channel. On June 18th Kokoshi, Aslani and thirty-six others stood trial in a Tirana cinema on charges of sabotage and spying. All were convicted and nine condemned to death. Albania apologised for the May 15th incident, but then declared a three-mile exclusion zone to foreign shipping, thereby effectively closing the Corfu channel which Britain regarded as an international waterway.

At the end of July the State Department noted that for Jacobs to remain in Albania was 'both futile and undignified'. He was receiving scant consideration, his sources of information were drying up and there was little to justify his mission. On October 10th he was replaced by a more junior official, George D. Henderson. Then on October 22nd Albania's relations with the Western allies received their coup de grâce. British destroyers sailed south from Corfu port in defiance of Albania's three-mile limit. While still in the channel the *Saumarez* and *Volage* struck mines and were seriously damaged, with forty-three men killed. This incident, known as the Corfu channel case, is still a bone of contention between Britain and Albania.

In early November another show trial started and this

time charges were made against United States mission employees, specifically that they conspired to sabotage a drainage project on Lake Maliq, near Korçë. On November 14th all the Americans left for Durazzo port, where the Albanian authorities subjected them to as many humiliations as they could invent. They refused to allow the Italian ship into the harbour, forcing them to spend two hours of seasickness in a tugboat on their way to where the ship lay ten miles offshore. They charged them one thousand dollars for the tugboat trip and they stole their luggage.

Henderson reported as soon as he arrived in Italy:

> Mission can reliably state that following methods of torture are used by Hoxha regime for purpose of obtaining false confessions: gashing leg, filling with salt, victims are known to have actually exhibited such wounds; electric current through decayed teeth or through bone in rear of ear; prolonged immersion in cold water up to neck; beating; splinters under fingernails; going through all preparations for execution even to firing blanks.

The United States and Britain began to lose patience with Albania. Hoxha's government was not only imposing a brutal dictatorship on the Albanian people, murdering opponents, falsifying elections and reneging on their autumn 1944 promise to submit to the people's will, but they had also by blowing up British warships and humiliating American diplomats offered gratuitous insults to the two democracies' prestige. It was an insult to all that the Western allies had done to liberate Albania from Nazi Germany. And, as if this was not enough, they were now brazenly attacking one of the cornerstones of the wartime agreements with the Soviet Union, a matter to which Stalin had set his mark, the decision that Greece would remain inside the Western sphere of influence and retain a non-communist government.

In December 1944 communist forces overran most of

Greece, as they did in Albania, and their victory was only frustrated by vigorous British intervention. Forced to disband their armies in February 1946, they went underground and the following year relaunched a full-scale guerilla war. Britain, to whose care Greece had been assigned by the three victorious allies, had commitments elsewhere, was no longer able to assist, so passed the torch to the United States. On March 12th, 1947, the US president announced what was to be known as the Truman Doctrine, informing Congress that in future it would be his policy to assist free peoples threatened 'by armed minorities or by outside pressures'. Three months later the Marshall Plan was launched. On October 21st, 1947, the UN General Assembly set up a special committee to investigate allegations that the Greek rebels under Markos Vafiades were being equipped and provided with safe havens by the governments of Albania, Bulgaria and Yugoslavia.

The Soviet Union and her allies took no part in the committee's work and they complained loudly when it reported in mid-1948 that Greece's three northern neighbours had indeed been succouring communist rebels. The committee noted that Albania was the most guilty of all, that Greek partisans 'made attacks from Albanian territory against the Greek national army in Greek territory', while Albania showed 'tolerance' to rebels entering the country to prepare these expeditions.[10]

'The very fate of my country is at stake,' said Greek representative Constantine Tsaldaris in the subsequent United Nations debate on November 22nd, 1948. American representative John Foster Dulles accused the three countries of 'the use of violence to make their views prevail'. The committee's British representative reported to the Foreign Office: 'The real villain of the piece is Albania. The guerilla HQ is in Greece on the eastern shore of Lake Mikra Prespa, conveniently placed for communication with Albania . . . We feel that a stern condemnation of Albania will be the best policy . . . Such a condemnation may prepare the ground for any future action against Albania by the United States and ourselves.'[11]

Guy Menant, French minister in Tirana, was now the main source of the few dismal scraps of information about Albania that reached the Western world. In September 1947 after a journey to Valona, Gjirokaster and along the Greek frontier to Konitsa he wrote of desolation, lack of cultivation and villages in ruins, with peasants working under the supervision of young armed men brought in from other parts of the country. He saw many Russian technicians.[12]

He also reported a mass trial of twenty-four American and British 'spies'. The proceedings, which were relayed to loudspeakers in the square outside the Tirana cinema that served as a courtroom, included noisy participation by the young men who formed the hand-picked audience: applause for the prosecuting counsel, catcalls for the accused and loud cries to the presiding judge calling for the death penalty. Three of the accused were hanged, thirteen shot and the rest imprisoned.[13]

Commander E. R. D. Sworder, who was allowed into Albania in January 1949 with the International Court mission investigating the Corfu channel case, reported, 'It is hard for a person brought up in the Western world to believe that such a form of civilisation as is practised in Albania today could really exist – a country where religion is frowned upon, where only government employees and members of the forces get a meat ration and 76 per cent of the population suffer from tuberculosis.' As they flew out of Albania his Swedish colleague Commodore S. A. Foreshell said, 'I have never been so glad to leave a country in my life. I think we have had a glimpse of hell.'[14]

This was the year in which the Cold War began to grip. In February 1948 the communists gained control of the Prague police and orchestrated a violent purge of non-communist influences in public life. On March 10th foreign minister Jan Masaryk was found dead in the courtyard of his house. It was announced that he committed suicide, but generally assumed that he had been murdered. On May 30th elections were held without opposition candidates and Czechoslovakia disappeared into the Soviet empire.

On June 24th the Soviet authorities in Berlin cut off all surface communication with the western zones of Germany, leaving only the air corridors. For a year the United States (mainly) and Britain supplied West Berlin's every need by aircraft at a cost of 224 million dollars. In China the communist armies of Mao Tse-tung were continuously victorious, poised by the end of the year to sweep away the nationalist government.

At the same time Władysław Gomułka, Poland's semi-independent communist leader, was replaced by a Soviet vassal and the same process of absorption was begun in Yugoslavia. However, on this occasion Stalin was unsuccessful. Yugoslavia's armed forces and police were men who had fought with Tito in the hills and expelled the German occupying armies themselves, without Soviet help. They had won power not as Soviet nominees but as conquerors in battle. Stalin had not made them and so could not easily break them either. Nevertheless, he resolved to do his worst. In June 1948 he expelled Yugoslavia from the Cominform, the organisation of communist states, labelling Tito's heresy as the Soviet Union's devil of the moment.

Albania was the country most affected. For five years Tito had behaved, as he liked to put it, like Enver Hoxha's elder brother, advising his partisans, guiding his policies, providing him with technicians and teachers as well as the food and manufactured goods that Albania conspicuously lacked. At the end of July reports from Guy Menant in Tirana mentioned 'general uneasiness' and a purge of officials, with every employee required to answer questions on his reaction to Tito's rebellion. Yugoslavs were leaving the country and the pro-Yugoslav interior minister Koci Xoxe was at loggerheads with other government leaders and about to be arrested.[15]

Menant also referred to the 'miserable conditions' in which the people lived. War was the only thing they had to look forward to, he wrote, since it would give them the chance to overthrow the Hoxha regime: 'He [Menant] stated that the arrival on the frontier of sizeable numbers of Allied troops would be the signal for a spontaneous uprising throughout Albania.'[16] By September he was writing of a Yugoslav-inspired 'insurrection' and 'guerilla activity' among the Shala and Hoti tribes of the north. And yet, he added, Hoxha was still helping the communist rebels against the Greek government and many Greek-speaking Albanians were fighting with them.[17]

The pieces of the puzzle were coming together to form a picture, an idea in the minds of Western decision-makers that perhaps Albania was not such an unimportant country after all. Before 1948 it was no more than an outpost of Stalin's empire, but by the end of the year this narrow little country, wedged between rebel Yugoslavia and civil-war-torn Greece, with Italy only fifty-five miles across the straits recovering from the trauma of her April 1948 elections, seemed to have become the key to many strategies, a Soviet strongpoint cut off from the rest of the bloc, a danger to its three non-Soviet-controlled neighbours far greater than its population of little more than a million might indicate. And, it seemed, this valuable prize was there for the taking, a poverty-stricken land torn by discontent and internal strife, suddenly deprived of its most important ally, a ripe peach hanging on its own at the end of the branch.

It was the moment of action for those angry Englishmen who had fought in Albania and seen, they believed, the nationalist cause betrayed. Julian Amery visited Greece in mid-1948 and returned to London with the germ of a plan:

> I hadn't realised how close the communists were to bringing down the Greek government. I had made some study of guerilla movements from 1939 to 1945 and it was clear

> to me that the only way to defeat them is to strike at the safe harbours that they often have on the other side of frontiers, either by hot pursuit, which is more normal, or by stirring up a guerilla movement against the government providing the harbour.

Amery's father was no longer in government. Churchill was leader of the opposition and Anthony Eden shadow foreign secretary. Still, they had served with the Labour ministers in the wartime coalition and they knew them well personally, especially prime minister Clement Attlee and foreign secretary Ernest Bevin. Amery himself had stood unsuccessfully in the 1945 general election and was Conservative candidate for Preston North. He also had friends from SOE days who had transferred to the Secret Intelligence Service. So he was well placed to pass on his thoughts to men of power and influence. On his return from Greece he began feeding Conservative leaders and SIS officers the idea that it was time for retaliation against Stalin's aggressive activity in Europe.

He expressed these same ideas publicly too in an article in the London journal *Time and Tide*. Greece was bleeding to death, he wrote. The fields untilled, the mines not in production, the towns full of penniless refugees from battle areas. The collective will of the Greek nation was flagging and the state in danger of collapse. There was only one answer to the problem – retaliation against the aggressor. It was time to give Stalin a taste of his own medicine.

What form was this retaliation to take? Amery had an answer:

> The position of the Albanian state is particularly precarious. Albania is Markos's main base, but it is separated from the rest of the Cominform bloc by deviationist Yugoslavia. It is desperately short of food, a number of political outlaws are still in the mountains, and news of recent purges suggests that the Albanian communist

> party is deeply divided between Stalinists and Titoists. In the face of a popular revolt the regime would be hard put to defend itself, let alone to continue its support of Markos.[18]

Amery's ideas struck a sympathetic chord with British ministers and officials, many of whom thought it was time for Britain and the United States to take some initiative against the Soviet adversary, to hit back at him where he was vulnerable instead of standing idly by and allowing him to swallow country after country. The mood was right: at about this time Britain launched a 'vigorous information offensive' on the basis of ideas put forward by Labour's junior Foreign Office minister Christopher Mayhew. A magazine called *Freedom First* was paid for out of secret British funds and a special body known as Information Research Department was set up to arrange similar projects. Mayhew recalls, 'It had to be secret. At that time millions of people, including most Labour parliamentarians, were singing the praises of dear old Uncle Joe.'[19]

Mayhew made speeches at the United Nations attacking the Soviet human rights record. He spoke of a country where retirement pensions were not high enough to support life, where old people were forced either to depend on their children or to work until they died. He estimated the October 1948 Soviet slave-labour population at five million, comparing it with Tsarist Russia's figure of only 169,367 prisoners in 1913. Soviet industrial progress had only been possible, he claimed, through the toil and misery of this vast army of unpaid workers.[20]

A new bureaucratic machine known as the Russia Committee was set up to plan and coordinate Britain's riposte. It was mainly a Foreign Office body, although representatives of the defence ministries and secret services also attended. Gladwyn Jebb, its chairman during 1948–9, confirms the committee's 'considerable influence on our policy towards the Soviet Union during a rather critical period'. NATO and the Marshall Plan were being established. Winston Churchill was privately urging the United States to seek a showdown with Stalin and to remind him of America's sole ownership of the atomic bomb. War with Russia was thought extremely likely and one Cabinet minister, Herbert Morrison, predicted that it would break out in summer 1949. Such apocalyptic notions can be read here and there in the minutes of Russia Committee meetings.

Its 'Cold War Sub-Committee' declared as its primary objective the loosening of 'the Soviet hold on the orbit countries and ultimately enabling them to regain their independence'. This aim they would achieve by 'promoting civil discontent, internal confusion and possible strife in the satellite countries'. The satellites would thus become a source of weakness to Russia rather than strength, a drain on her resources of expertise and manpower, an area so disaffected that large Soviet armies of occupation would be required even in wartime.[21]

Albania was first mentioned at a committee meeting called on November 25th, 1948, to consider other ways of fighting the Cold War and attended by a galaxy of future ambassadors, Gladwyn Jebb, Ivone Kirkpatrick, Roger Makins, William Hayter, Robin Hankey and Frank Roberts as well as by air force chief, Lord Tedder. It was at this meeting that the use of subversion against communist governments along the lines of wartime SOE operations was first considered seriously and Albania was put forward as the most suitable target.

Tedder said that the aim should be to win the Cold War, by which he meant the overthrow of the Soviet regime, within five years. Then Ivone Kirkpatrick brought up the subject of Albania. He did this, he said, partly for financial reasons. Britain was in no position to launch a large-scale subversive operation against an important country. But might it not be possible to start a civil war in Albania that would produce a situation similar to that prevailing in

Greece? Everyone knew, he added, that there was opposition to the communist regime. It ought to be possible to exploit it.

The committee made no specific conclusion about Albania, but they did decide 'that our aim should certainly be to liberate the countries within the Soviet orbit by any means short of war'.[22] There is nothing in the available British records explaining how this general conclusion became a clear governmental decision to remove Hoxha's regime in Albania, but it seems clear that the Russia Committee's proposal was soon translated into action, encouraged as it was by Amery's expert lobbying and the strong feelings of others who had served in Albania. Although there is no record available, it is presumed by those close to the project that towards the end of 1948 Ernest Bevin (on the advice of his Foreign Office subordinates, including SIS chief Stewart Menzies) gave the official go-ahead as far as Britain was concerned. All the lobbying and discussions had finally paid off.

The officially-sanctioned, if small-scale, military and political operation had as its principal aim the end of Albania's communist government. In the process Albania would be punished for the Corfu channel incident and for making her land available to Greek communists. Then there was the idealistic desire to steer a European country, one which US President Woodrow Wilson had personally sponsored, into the democratic fold.

But the grander design was not forgotten. If the smallest and weakest link in the Soviet bloc, a link now cut off from the rest of the chain, could be turned from an unfriendly into a friendly country then Stalin, too, could be punished – for his destruction of Czechoslovakia's democracy and for his attempts to starve West Berlin, for his crude oppression of 'nationalist' figures in the Soviet bloc, and his perfidy in sponsoring rebellion against the Greek government. It would also frustrate his scheme for controlling the Adriatic's entrance (he was equipping Saseno Island with submarines and rockets, based on the German V-2 models, capable of reaching the Italian mainland). Finally it might also deter him from further encroachments and to warn him off any clumsy reaction to Tito's deviation.

Ernest Bevin, nevertheless, retained the view, as his then private secretary Frank Roberts confirms, that the Russia Committee's far-reaching general conclusions were over-ambitious, hence it made better sense to mount the policy of retaliation on a modest basis only and in a small, little-known country – at least at the outset – partly for financial reasons, but also to avoid any adverse public reaction if the secret leaked out.

There were many, it is true, who would have upheld the project, from the moral as well as the political point of view. Julian Amery, for instance, has no doubts: 'You can't apply the Marquess of Queensberry rules to one side and not the other. Stalin was trying to overthrow the pro-Western government in Athens, so I think we had every right to try and overthrow the pro-Soviet government in Tirana, or indeed in Sofia if we so wished.' He agrees, though, that it must have taken great courage for Bevin to have sanctioned such a plan. Many members of the Labour party would have been shocked at the idea of a British socialist government using the secret service to subvert and abolish a new revolutionary republic with a gallant anti-Nazi war record.

There was another problem. Britain had the goodwill, the expertise and several possible bases in the Mediterranean only a few hundred miles from the target. But she was in the throes of post-war austerity and she did not have the money. McLean remembers one man from the Foreign Office advising him sternly. 'Church mice do not start wars.'

The Russia Committee therefore agreed on December 16th 'that there could be no question of taking action without coordination with the United States government'.[23] They might also consult the Canadian government, but not the European allies. They were worried only that 'there was lack of coordination of [American] subversive activities' and that, in William Hayter's view, the Americans were not always as forthcoming as he could have wished. On February 13th, 1949, Frank Roberts told the committee that Ernest Bevin had agreed on a plan 'to detach Albania from the orbit'.[24] He proposed to consult Prime Minister Attlee on how this could best be done 'in consultation with any other government departments concerned'.

Hayter was told to square the American side and a month later he flew to Washington as leader of a delegation of Foreign Office and SIS men, including Gladwyn Jebb of the Russia Committee and Lord Jellicoe, the British embassy's Balkan specialist. At a three-day conference with their American opposite numbers, led by Robert Joyce of the State Department and OPC chief Frank Wisner, they discussed an entire programme of Anglo-American intelligence cooperation in the face of the Soviet threat.

An American who was present at the talks recalls much discussion about the West's inability to prosecute the Cold War. They simply did not have the proper machinery to carry out covert operations overseas. In the lead-up to the April 1948 Italian elections, which were very important for the Western world, the United States had been reduced to handing out large sums of money to the party they wanted to win, the Christian Democrats, with little or no supervision. They talked about how to develop a more subtle approach, in particular in Italy and Yugoslavia, two important Cold War battlegrounds. The Albanian project was simply another item on the agenda and it was approved without undue debate.

The previous year the intelligence division of the US Army had reported that Albania enjoyed a strategic importance far out of proportion to its size or natural resources: 'It extends the Soviet sphere of influence to the Mediterranean, within easy reach of bases and communications lines of vital importance to the United Kingdom and the United States. There is evidence that the Soviets appreciate the value of the outpost for both defensive and offensive purposes . . . It could also provide a base for operations against Italy or Mediterranean shipping.'[25]

These were the sound defensive reasons for approving an operation designed to neutralise Soviet bases in Albania. The long-term forecast was more enticing still. A successful rebellion in Albania would boost the morale of anti-communists through the Soviet empire, encouraging them to believe that the West was ready to give them serious support, militarily as well as politically. It would be realistic, if the Albanian plan was successful, to talk of 'a chain reaction that would roll back the tide of Soviet imperialism'. Guerilla fighters would flourish in the fertile soil of communist poverty and oppression. The seeds would grow and eventually the fruit of counter-revolution in all eastern Europe would ripen.

Who then were these guerilla fighters to be? They could not be American or British subjects. There was no question of sending Amery, Smiley, Northrop, Hibberdine, Kemp and Simcox back into Albania to recruit their old friends from five years earlier against a different enemy. Such exploits were appropriate to the hot war, but not to the Cold War. Britain had agreed to organise a military operation in time of peace. This had to be kept secret and she could not expose her agents to capture in the field. The consequences of the capture of a British officer by the Tirana regime would be most embarrassing. The risk could not be taken.

There was, however, an alternative supply, the large number of Albanians who had left their homeland for Greece after the communist victory. Most of the royalist and Balli Kombëtar wartime resistance leaders were outside Albania, available for American or British service. Midhat Frasheri was in Turkey, Abas Ermenji in Greece, Said Kryeziu and Abas Kupi in Italy. There were several thousand Albanians in Italian refugee camps – Santa Maria di Leuca,

Cinecittà, Barletta and Reggio nell' Emilia. King Zog and his entourage were in Egypt.

It made sense therefore to restrict the American and British role in the affair and so preserve the two governments' capacity for plausible denial. They would sponsor the rebellion and the rebels, but take no active part in it on Albanian soil. They would organise the exile leaders into a political unit which would be publicised, and recruit through them young men for the project's secret military side. They would train them, equip them, deliver them into Albania and communicate with them, paying all the bills. If any were caught, they would disclaim all knowledge of them.

Britain took the lead in the project because of her background of involvement in Albania and the Balkans. She had a wealth of talent ready for recruitment, for instance Dayrell Oakley-Hill, who had helped run the Albanian gendarmerie under King Zog and spoke the language excellently. The United States had no such person. The operation's first American 'commander' James McCargar says, 'The expertise in the affair was 99 per cent British. They had so many people who had been there during the war, most of them young and intelligent. We only had American citizens of Albanian origin, none of them specialists in what we were trying to achieve.' Robert Low, the first American intelligence officer to approach problems in the field, agrees: 'At that stage it was entirely up to the British "cousins" to provide local knowledge and political guidance. Their secret service with its men who had served in SOE during the war were the world's experts in this kind of thing.'

McLean and Amery had kept in touch with their former Albanian comrades-in-arms, helping them through the first years of penniless, dispiriting exile. They raised the matter of the gold Abas Kupi had lent them when their funds ran out in 1944. The British authorities at first refused repayment, then offered to settle at the nominal rate of the gold sovereign, one pound a coin. McLean protested strongly:

'We were under an obligation to these people, nationally as well as personally. They saved British and American lives. If it had not been for the politics of the thing, they would have been given British medals. They certainly deserved them.' Eventually Abas Kupi was repaid the full amount out of secret funds.

They helped them with jobs and visas too, and through one particular crisis in 1947 when Hoxha put pressure on the Italian government for the forcible return of Albanian anti-communists, offering in exchange Italian prisoners from his own gaols. McLean recalls 'a great panic among our Albanian friends' when about fifteen were arrested and taken from place to place, including the famous Regina Coeli prison in Rome, then in early 1948 to the Fraschetti camp just outside the city. It was feared that some were going to be sacrificed. It was a difficult period, just before the April 1948 elections. The Left was particularly influential and the safety of Italian citizens was involved.

Bido Kuka was one of those in Fraschetti camp. He remembers the commandant promising the anti-communist prisoners that, if the Left won the elections, he would arm them and take to the hills with them. Orme Sargent also intervened with the Italian foreign office, at McLean's request, and shortly after the elections all Albanians were released. No wonder then that the four musketeers, having fought with the Albanian exiles in war and for them in peace, enjoyed their absolute trust.

In March 1949 McLean and Amery were told that their pleas for action against Hoxha had finally been heard. In a series of meetings during the weeks that followed they gave their valuable background information to the Foreign Office men involved – Orme Sargent, Charles Bateman and Anthony Rumbold – and to the appropriate secret intelligence officers from Broadway Buildings in London's St James's – operational wizard Harold Perkins, his deputy Jessica Aldridge and their old colleague from the Albanian resistance Alan Hare.

Frank Wisner flew to London and lunched with McLean at Buck's Club on April 14th. The question of a guerilla training base was discussed during the visit and the location first suggested was the United States's Whelus airbase in Libya. This was finally turned down for political reasons and the choice fell on the British island of Malta where there was an ideal location, Fort Bin Jema, a nineteenth-century castle with a moat deep enough to be used as a firing range. Wisner remarked, according to Kim Philby in his book *My Silent War*, 'Whenever we want to subvert any place, we find that the British own an island within easy reach.[26]

Two weeks later McLean discussed the plan over dinner with shadow foreign secretary Anthony Eden. All this time the leading Albanian exiles, including Ermenji and Frasheri, were slowly being assembled in Rome. McLean and Amery, it was agreed, would meet them in Rome and persuade them to cooperate. The armed men who were to go into Albania needed a political foundation, a government-in-exile that would unite all anti-communist Albanians and give the guerilla fighters some form of legitimacy. McLean and Amery were the only two Westerners capable of breaking through the barriers of mistrust and accomplishing such a delicate political task.

They needed an American, someone to show the Albanians that this was to be a joint operation. The OPC had no one of McLean's or Amery's experience, but shortly after the Washington agreement they sent for Robert Low, a US army reserve officer. He had been an intelligence officer in Western Europe during the last year of the war and then a *Time-Life* correspondent in Prague. He was also knowledgeable about the Balkans, especially Bulgaria, and had worked with the wartime Office of Strategic Services (OSS) in Cairo. 'I was not an unfamiliar face among members of the "old British firm",' he says. 'I knew nothing about Albania, but at that stage we were only going to help the British with finance and logistics. And I was to be living proof in our talks of the United States's commitment.'

The political side was covered. They then needed someone to run the military side, someone to train the young Albanians, someone with intimate knowledge of the country and people as well as the skills of guerilla warfare. There was really only one candidate for the job. David Smiley had stayed in the army as a professional and in early 1949 he was in Germany as second-in-command of his regiment, the Royal Horse Guards.

Perkins came over to consult Xan Fielding, his resident man in the north-east of the British zone, and together they drove to Smiley's regimental base for dinner. It was over a glass of brandy after dinner, Fielding remembers, that Perkins first spoke to Smiley about the Albanian plan. And it struck him as 'rather amateurish' that such a secret matter, the detail of which he had no need to know, should be discussed in his presence.

Smiley says, 'My colonel retired, but I was only thirty-two, so they said I was too young to take over. Just at that time Harold Perkins, my contact in the "firm" asked me if I would set up a training school in Malta and arrange for the infiltration of Albanian agents. I admit, I rather jumped at it.'

Perkins and his SIS had quickly acquired a trainer, a base and full political backing; soon they would have their 'off the peg' Albanian government and enough young volunteers to begin the battle. They now had to consider practical details. How were these agents to be put into the field? British intelligence favoured, as usual, the idea of a sea landing from a small boat. How then were they to find the boat and a reliable crew? They placed the matter in the hands of their SIS station chief in Athens, Pat Whinney, a former naval commander, a tall extrovert who had acquired a mountain of eastern Mediterranean experience.

It did not take Whinney long to nominate two men, Sam Barclay and John Leatham. Barclay was a painter, Leatham a writer. Both loved the sea and they had spent two years working for the British military mission in Athens running cargoes in an old trading ketch, the *Bessie*, for the benefit of Greek forces fighting the communist rebellion. In August 1948 they sold the *Bessie* and early the following month laid the keel for their new boat, the *Stormie Seas*.

Leatham says, 'I was twenty-five, Sam was twenty-nine. We both had an exciting time during the war. We weren't ready to settle down and we both wanted to get back to sea without admirals breathing down our necks. We were looking only for free adventure and a living, the ability to pay our bills in and out of port.' They hoped to have the boat ready for launching in November, but towards the end of that month Leatham recorded in a letter to his mother (November 27th) that they were having trouble with the chief shipwright: 'It is his fault that his estimation of the building costs has been surpassed by the actual expenses, but he is more than unwilling to accept the unhappy consequences of his own misjudgement and mismanagement.'

At this point Whinney stepped in. He had met the *Bessie* boys, as they were known, in July and had a high opinion of their usefulness. Towards the end of 1948 he explained to them that his superiors in SIS would very easily find a use for two good men and a good boat. He offered to help them out of their financial problem by taking over the cost of building the *Stormie Seas* and he agreed to install the very powerful engine. The Greek shipbuilders were told not to complete the boat, just to make her seaworthy. They would then take her to Malta under sail. The engine would be installed and the carpentry work completed on the slipway of Manuel Island at the British taxpayer's expense.

Their remuneration was set at fifty pounds a month each, tax-free plus expenses. 'We were paying the price of victory,' says Leatham. 'Britain was short of money and the secret service was under instructions to be cheese-paring.' The salary did not take into account the danger of their work. It was less than they would have got through a commercial charter. Still, as Leatham explains, it was a case where patriotism and sense of duty counted more than money:

'We were young, but not too young to know where we belonged. We didn't know much about Albania, but we knew about Greece; we were fond of Greece and we didn't like what the communists were doing to her in 1948–9, especially carrying children off away from their parents. Some of the children were being taken across into Albania.'

During November the boat was painted its distinctive blue-green colour. On December 15th she was launched and Leatham wrote: 'We slid gracefully down into the sea and rode like a swan on the windswept waters. *Stormie Seas* is a lovely sight, but she will be finer still when the masts are in and the rigging up. We are very pleased both with her and to find ourselves afloat again.'

During the first days of 1949 the two young Englishmen made their final preparations, including the difficult task of obtaining an exit permit for their Greek boatman Dino Mavros, who was of military age. Pat Whinney and his wife Maria came on board on January 24th. The days were marred only by a dispute with SIS's accountants in Athens. Barclay says, 'They queried our list of expenses. It infuriated us, because we had put in for what we spent on food and supplies, no more and no less. They said it was rather a lot and they were prepared to pay 75 per cent. John became very English and upright. He asked them how they dared question his word. They paid the full amount.'

The *Stormie Seas* left Piraeus on February 18th. First they were becalmed and took four days to travel thirty-six miles to the eastern end of the Corinth canal. Then they had to be towed through the canal, since they had no engine. Head winds delayed them again and they were towed into Patras in western Greece. Leatham wrote on March 4th: 'So far we are well pleased with the *Stormie Seas*'s performance, though we have yet to discover how she will behave in heavy weather in open seas.'

They soon found out. Shortly after they put into the Mediterranean a storm got up and cracked the foremast, forcing them to pull down sails. The mast became insecure after the bobstay, which runs from the end of the bowsprit down to water level, cracked at deck level. This meant that the forestay, running from the peak of the foremast down to the end of the bowsprit, was no longer forming a secure triangle, so it began to whip around in the heavy seas.

The foremast was in danger of falling on the crew's heads and entangling them in shrouds. They carried on as best they could with a reefed sail on the mainmast and reached Gallipoli in southern Italy, where they crawled in for repairs. The mast was removed, the section below the crack sawn off, then repositioned. It meant that they did not reach Malta until March 31st. The voyage from Piraeus had taken six weeks. They left Mavros to supervise the work on Manuel Island and flew to England to be briefed by SIS about their assignment.

They too were taken under the protection of Harold Perkins, the ebullient and legendary 'alchemist' of the Albanian operation whose picture still hangs in the 'rogues gallery' of the Special Forces Club in Knightsbridge. Perks, as he was known, had been a master mariner, then graduated from Prague university as an engineer. He lived in Poland, where he ran a textile factory, and when war broke out escaped with the British military mission through Rumania. By the war's end he was responsible for SOE operations in Poland, Czechoslovakia and Hungary.

It was his affection for these three countries, all of which disappeared into the Soviet empire shortly after the war, that strengthened his anti-communist motivation in 1948–9. He was, Barclay recalls, 'anxious to do the Soviet Union down at every turn'. He retained close links with émigré Poles in particular and his name was mentioned in Polish show trials of 'spies' and 'traitors' in the Stalinist period. His role as the Albanian operation's guiding hand was one out of a wide range of secret anti-Soviet subversive activities.

Their Broadway briefing was sparse. 'We were told that the less we knew the better,' says Barclay. They were going to have to bring their boat close to the Albanian shore.

They were the only British men involved who risked being captured. Barclay was due to be married in a few weeks and his wife Eileen would be with them on the trip. Perkins told them what they needed to know and nothing more.

On May 2nd he flew to Athens with McLean and Alan Hare. A few days later Amery joined them. Meanwhile Smiley was assembling his team of instructors in the art of sabotage and guerilla warfare.

The 'four musketeers' were back in action. They had fought the Germans together, after which they had all been unceremoniously bundled out of Albania on the orders of men over whose judgement and loyalty they nursed deep doubts, leaving a people they had come to admire in the hands of vicious dictators who were now the slavish allies of Britain's adversary in the Cold War. They were delighted to be given the chance to resume the fray.

3 Athens, Rome, Cairo and Malta

The British secret service's amateur tradition knows no clearer example than that of the unpaid odyssey that laid the Albanian affair's foundations. In the spring of 1949 McLean and Amery were invited to become special advisers to the government and to go on a tour of the Mediterranean's Albanian exile centres. The aim was to create a political base from which the military subversion of the Hoxha government would be launched. The two men had recently been selected as Conservative parliamentary candidates, but they were employed by no government department, they worked on an expenses-only basis and they had no official standing whatever.

Amery says, 'The secret services asked me to set up the organisation for an Albanian counter-revolution and I was glad to do it. I wasn't a professional, but they were my friends and I wanted to help them.' Amery and McLean enjoyed a relationship of trust with the exile leaders and this goodwill was extremely valuable to SIS and CIA/OPC at this early stage.

There were complicated diplomatic problems to be solved before any guerilla operation could begin. The first was the Albanian exiles' disunity. The three main political groups were at loggerheads and hardly communicated. The royalists, notably King Zog and his military commanders Abas Kupi and Nuçi Kota, were by definition opposed to the republican Balli Kombëtar – Frasheri, Ermenji, Zef Pali, Hasan Dosti and Vasil Andoni. And both were the sworn adversaries of the National Independents, known as

Independenza, mainly Catholics from the north-west of the country and naturally pro-Italian, many of whom had worked with the Italians during the war. The Kossovars in the north-east, led by the Kryeziu family, were another identifiable group. And there were a few men, such as Ihsan Toptani, who were influential through family prestige and individual ability.

These political factions were united in their fervent opposition to communism but in very little else. They all proclaimed their belief in parliamentary democracy, but they had little experience of democracy in practice and often their words were designed to impress their Western allies rather than each other. Another unifying force was the general Albanian distrust of neighbouring countries that sought to annex their territory. Every party resented Greek aspirations to possess southern Albania, what the Greeks call northern Epirus, and there was no Albanian who did not resent the fact that Yugoslavia had reannexed Kossovo and its million Albanian-speaking inhabitants after the war.

However, on most other important issues, such as land reform, the monarchy and the attitude of foreign powers, there was no agreement whatever between the parties. The US embassy in Rome reported in December 1948 that relations between them were bound to be strained, because 'each was originally established for the primary purpose of destroying the others'.[27]

The Greek territorial claim was another source of disunity and a threat to the operation's success. Greek cooperation was an essential part of the West's plans, but Greece was interested more in retaking northern Epirus, many of whose people spoke Greek, than in establishing pro-Western democracy in an independent Albania. It was a litmus test of Greek patriotism and although in 1949 there were many in Greece who saw the claim as unrealistic, there was no political figure who would ever have dared deny it publicly. And if there was one thing guaranteed to frustrate any effort to remove Hoxha's regime, even to make Hoxha popular, it was the idea that the West was plotting with Greece to deprive Albania of 20 per cent of her territory, perhaps even to partition the country between Greece and Yugoslavia.

This was the message that Amery put to Greek politicians during the first leg of his journey in May 1949. He met Themistocles Sophoulis and Stilianos Gonotas, veterans of the Venizelos movement, and liberal leader George Papandreou. He says, 'I tried to convince them that their territorial claim was counter-productive. They were in mortal danger from their own communist rebels and a policy of annexation just did not make sense. A policy of retaliation did make sense.' He and McLean flew to Yanina near the Albanian border and spoke to the northern Epirus committee.

The third problem was Greece's attitude to the anti-Hoxha conspiracy. Greek intelligence agents were already active in Albania, promoting their cause among the Greek-speaking population. This could never be made public. If it were, Greece would be seriously embarrassed. All the more reason then was there to make sure that there would be no confusion over this new British and American plan of subversion. The British radio listening post was going to be in Corfu on Greek territory. Greece was the guerilla fighters' only safe haven of retreat and in due course it would become their point of departure too. There would be confusion and recrimination if Greece was not put in the picture.

There was only one person who could authorise such a sensitive and potentially embarrassing use of Greek resources – Field Marshal Alexander Papagos, the Greek army commander and power behind the government of a weak prime minister, Alexander Diomedes. The question was how to approach him? He was busy and this was not a matter to be discussed with colleagues or secretaries present. Amery solved the problem by obtaining through an old SOE comrade-in-arms, a well-known Turkish arms dealer, an introduction to one of Papagos's closest friends, Bodosis Athenisiades, known as 'Bodosaki', an arms dealer on the grand scale and one of Greece's richest men.

Amery and McLean took Bodosaki to lunch at a taverna outside Athens where there was no chance of their being overheard. Amery says:

> Over two or three hours I explained to Bodosaki what was in our minds and convinced him. He said he would go to the Field Marshal at once and talk to him about it. He said, 'I wonder how I'm going to let you know.' He asked when I was leaving and I said, 'If not tomorrow, then the day after.' And he said, 'That's time enough. If it's no I'll leave one bottle of brandy in your room at the hotel. If it's yes, I'll leave six.' I found six.

They discussed the project with British ambassador Clifford Norton, then with SIS station chief Pat Whinney, his deputies Eric McCloud and John Baddesley, his secretary Iris Riddle, as well as with Panayotis Pipenelis, secretary-general at the Greek foreign office. According to McLean's notes, the Greeks they spoke to admitted that victory in the civil war would hardly be possible without closing the Albanian border. 'The present regime in Albania, or the guerilla camps at least, must be liquidated,' they told him. Southern Albania, where the main opposition was Balli Kombëtar, was therefore the priority area and it made sense, since decisive encounters with Markos's forces were believed imminent, to recruit Balli supporters in the first instance for training and infiltration near the border area.

The next step was to discuss it with the Balli military commander Abas Ermenji, who had been in Greece since the end of 1945, first in prison in Salonika and then in a flat in Piraeus. Ermenji was treated with suspicion by the Greek authorities because of the Greek-Albanian territorial dispute. For some months he had wanted to travel to Rome and had been refused permission. The proposals that his two British friends put to him gave him the chance of getting out of Athens and back into action.

The British did not, while recruiting Ermenji, emphasise their concern over the Greek civil war or the need to launch some symbolic act of retaliation against the Soviet Union. Albanians were not going to be asked to risk their lives on Greece's behalf. If they had been approached on this basis, they would have refused. McLean, Hare and Amery persuaded Ermenji, though he needed little persuasion, with an exclusively Albanian argument, the fact that his country's existence was in peril as a result of Yugoslavia's expulsion from the Soviet bloc. Albania had become a country without defence, a power vacuum, and she might well be partitioned. It was therefore his duty to act now, to rally his supporters, to anticipate Greek and Yugoslav ambitions. And at the same time his country would be liberated from the communists: 'They told me that I was the only person who could take such an initiative and make it good. I accepted.'

Ermenji wanted the agreement to be confirmed by Frasheri, the party leader, so Frasheri was duly brought from Istanbul to Rome. And within a few days Ermenji too found himself issued with a ticket, a forged passport and the name of a 'friend' who would ensure his safe passage through Athens airport. On May 18th McLean and Perkins also flew to Rome. On May 20th they began a series of meetings with the two Balli leaders. Their first requirement, Perkins explained, was thirty young men suitable for training in Malta by their other old friend David Smiley.

It did not take Ermenji and Andoni long to pick the men from various Italian refugee camps in the Naples area. The main problem, Ermenji recalls, was the young men's keenness to volunteer and their anger when it emerged that only thirty would be allowed to take part. Neither Ermenji nor his men understood why men were being recruited on such a puny scale: 'Everyone wanted to go. We could have got hundreds of Albanians from Italy, thousands from the Albanian community in Turkey, and others too – Bulgarians, Croatians and Poles. We should have sent thousands in, a force big enough to create whole areas of opposition to the regime.'

In spite of their reservations, Frasheri, Ermenji and Andoni did what they were asked. Bardhyl Gerveshi was one of the first to be recruited. He had left Albania as a seventeen-year-old boy at the end of 1947 with his friend Haki Gaba, creeping their way from Gjirokaster through the mountains towards the border: 'Our main problem was water. We never went near springs or streams in the mountains. We collected snow in an army ground sheet and every day used the sun to melt it down into an old tin. Every evening we went into a farmhouse and stole some food, trying not to show that we had been there, in case they reported us.'

Sometimes they stole a sheep or a goat, always two or three hours before nightfall, so that they would be away and in a cave in a different valley by the time its loss was discovered. They spent the last two days climbing their way through a forest with no food at all. After crossing the border the Greeks interrogated them in the northern town of Yanina, then took them to Hadjikyriakon camp near Athens, from which they were flown to Bari and taken by train to Cinecittà refugee camp.

Gerveshi says, 'Andoni and Ermenji didn't ask for volunteers. They knew who their party members were and who was suitable for the job. As for myself, there was no question of refusing. When your life is devoted to your country, you are prepared to do anything to help it.' There was no shortage of this type of enthusiasm and patriotic fervour. There was, however, a lack of education and leadership potential. There were no officers among the thirty recruits, no one with any academic or military training. Several were unable to write and others were physically too weak for the tasks that they were going to be asked to fulfil. The Albanian monarchist leader, Gaqi Gogo, a former decathlon champion, is especially critical of these original recruits' physique. They were, he says, men with narrow chests and necks like chickens.

Stormie Seas, the boat that was due to take them into action, was by now on the slips at Manuel Island in Malta. On May 15th Leatham was in England standing as best man at Barclay's marriage to Eileen and by the end of the month he was back in Malta complaining in letters to his mother about lack of progress: 'Thursday is of course Ascension Day and no work will be done. Friday is pay day and the maties [workmen] knock off earlier than ever. And they never work Saturdays . . . Work aboard marches ahead, but it is a slow march as for a funeral.'

On May 23rd Alan Hare left for London, to be replaced the following day by another SIS officer, John Hibberdine, an 'old Albanian hand' who had served with the resistance among Catholic tribes in the north. On May 25th McLean and Amery returned to London and during the next few days visited various offices to report on their mission. They saw Dick Brooman-White and Tommy Last in Broadway Buildings, Anthony Rumbold and Charles Bateman in the Foreign Office, Harold Macmillan in the Turf Club.

Robert Low, the American representative, came to London from Washington in early June and within a few days he was steeped in the plan's political and operational detail. He met all those involved and was even granted a short interview with SIS boss Stewart Menzies. 'They had obviously given a lot of thought to the planning,' he says. 'The various papers were well done. They made sense and they were feasible. I never thought it was going to be a "cinch", but I certainly thought it worth a try. If I hadn't, I'd have said so at the time.'

He was influenced, he recalls, by Albania's isolated and vulnerable state. She had no common border with the Soviet Union and would be hard to reinforce. And he was impressed both by the expert knowledge that the SIS had been able to assemble on the basis of British wartime experience and by the SIS's emotional commitment to the idea of liberating Albania from the communists. Several career SIS officers including Hare and Hibberdine, had served there during the war. They still smarted from the humiliation of their expulsion from the country by Hoxha's partisans, men with whom they had fought against Nazi Germany. They were anxious to settle accounts with these cut-throats who had accepted British advice and equipment, then used it to treat Britain with contempt.

Low was impressed too, as was McCargar, by the strength of British feeling about the Corfu channel incident. There was no reason, they explained to the Americans, why Britain should tolerate having her warships blown up on the high seas by the gang of murderers who made up the Hoxha regime. At one point Dick Brooman-White suggested, only half-jokingly, that if SIS were to arrange another explosion on another of His Majesty's ships in the Corfu area it would provide an excellent pretext for formal British and American armed intervention.

Low played only a small part in the planning. The United States was for the moment still the junior partner. His job was to observe, to report back and to provide, as he recalls, Greeks and Albanians with living proof of America's solidarity with Britain in the enterprise, especially when it came to the promise of financial backing. On June 24th he and Robert Minor, another American intelligence officer, flew to Rome with the British team to conclude their talks with the exiles.

It was a very difficult negotiation. Low remembers working lunches in a restaurant in the Borghese Gardens overlooking the Vatican, followed by meetings with the Albanians in the open air, sometimes sitting Turkish-style crosslegged on the ground. It was before the days of directional microphones, so they could talk in the gardens without fear of being overheard. And it would have been easy to tell if they were being followed. They also sometimes met in two 'safe houses' that were regularly 'swept' for hidden devices. Their job was to persuade the Albanians to agree on a president and executive committee, men who would form the country's government after liberation.

They had to overcome the rivalry and distrust between royalist and republican, Christian and Moslem, northerner and southerner. They had to sort out the problem of the many Albanians, among them some of the best educated, who had collaborated with Italian rule. The worst problems of all were the family rows, the blood feuds that divided whole communities, often resulting in murderous attacks. Several times, Low remembers, they got to the edge of agreement, only to find that one piece of the Chinese puzzle would not fit, whereupon the whole complicated structure fell apart.

Abas Ermenji was particularly hard to convince. Amery remembers his manner in 1944 as 'pedantic', that 'he seemed always to be worrying about himself',[28] and five years later he had not mellowed. As the Balli's young military commander, fiercely anti-royalist, he was instinctively hostile to the Anglo-American plan for an agreement with Zog. He saw the ex-King as insignificant and took the view that he should have spent the war fighting in Albania, rather than living with his family in Henley-on-Thames, England.

Ermenji, a fighting man, also disliked the idea of yielding first place to Frasheri, his party's seventy-year-old intellectual president. He had come to Italy from Greece illegally and he feared that Albanians of the pro-Italian Independence party were plotting to have him arrested. Eventually, using this as a pretext, the British removed him from Rome to the international city of Trieste, where his influence on the negotiations was more remote, and he could be kept under observation by Archie Lyall, British information officer in Trieste and an SIS member. Even so there were terrible rows about party and status. The British and Americans told him that, if he did not moderate his stance, they would abandon Albania to the whims of her two neighbours. Ermenji replied that in that case he would offer his services to the Soviet embassy, that he would go to any lengths to preserve Albania's independence.

King Zog's participation in the committee was not possible. There was no way by which his position could allow him to take part in any Albanian representative body except as its leader. And everyone knew that, if he were to be made chairman of such a body, the Balli men would withdraw from it at once. On the other hand his acquiescence, his acceptance of the political and military plan, was essential, because if he denounced it, the royalists would all have denounced it too and abandoned it. This was the complicated political juggling act that Amery, Low, McLean, Hare, Perkins and Minor had to maintain without dropping a single ball.

The Western negotiators saw the Albanians as argumentative and petty. It is fair to record, though, that the Albanians had their legitimate concerns. Many were disturbed at the idea of becoming American and British agents, that they were being bought by foreigners to attack an Albanian government, even a loathsome Albanian government, and they did not relish the role of guinea-pig in some great experiment that concerned not only Albania. Conflicts of interest between them and the two big powers were bound to arise soon, they thought, and in those conflicts how would they ever have the power to gain the upper hand?

'Those were the golden days,' recalls Vasil Andoni. 'They promised us the moon. They were going to protect us from our greedy neighbours and free us from the communists at the same time.' The Albanians were astute enough to realise, though, that the United States and Britain had other concerns too. And Frasheri made sure that he was not being 'bought' by insisting that all money advanced for the operation was a loan to the future Albanian government. Full accounts would be kept and after liberation the American and British money would be repaid.

It took many days of intensive discussion in Rome to work out a political compromise. In the end the best that could be obtained for the royalists was the chairmanship of the military junta, the secret body that would control military operations. Abas Kupi, the King's nominee, was appointed junta chairman, with Ermenji and Said Kryeziu as his deputies. Gaqi Gogo, the King's secretary, was made junta secretary and also secretary to the Albanian National Committee executive, a public political body set up to put free Albania's case before the world. The chairmanship of this executive, the main job, was given to the Balli leader Midhat Frasheri. Agreement on these points was reached on July 7th.

The final problem was to persuade King Zog to accept this compromise. Obviously he was not going to find it agreeable. Any proposal to set up a sort of shadow government, which was what the Westerners had in mind, with someone other than himself as president or chairman, was from his point of view a usurpation of royal prerogative. Zog's position was that he had never abdicated, that he had left his country with the agreement of its Parliament and people in the face of foreign aggression, that in spite of the Italian and German occupations, in spite of the illegal communist takeover and the bogus elections, he remained Albania's King. And this fact was based not on politics, but on continuity and legality. This is why 'Legaliteti' was the name of his movement.

King Zog had moved his household to Egypt in 1946. He was received by King Farouk with the hospitality appropriate to a fellow Moslem and fellow monarch. He, Queen Geraldine and Prince Leka lived first at the Hotel Manor House at Giza near the Pyramids, then at a large villa in Ramleh, Alexandria. The King's entourage was considerable. Only one of his sisters, Adile, remained in London. The other five – Nafije, Senie, Muzejen, Maxhide and Ruhije – lived with the King and Queen in the villa.

Prince Leka attended Alexandria's Victoria School,

which was run along British lines. He was also taught by a Swiss governess, Elizabeth Aegerter, who was also the Queen's personal assistant. The King's main adviser was his minister of court, Sotir Martini. He had his secretary Gaqi Gogo and his royal guard under the command of a colonel, Hysen Selmani, which included Zenel Shehu and Halil Branica. There were maids, a driver and other servants.

Post-war Alexandria, situated as it was between the poverty of Asia and the austerity of Europe's devastation, provided an oasis of good living for many wealthy exiles, several of them royal. Apart from the Albanian house there was King Simeon of Bulgaria and his mother Joanna; and, embarrassingly, King Victor Emmanuel of Italy. It was his armies, after all, that had invaded Albania and deposed King Zog in 1939. It was a diplomatic problem that several wise men took pains to solve and eventually, for the sake of peace in Alexandrian high society, if for no other reason, a truce was declared between the two enemy kings.

Gaqi Gogo recalls:

> We worked from nine in the morning until three or four at night, all the time planning for the liberation of Albania. It was hard work, but we did have time for games after dinner, bridge and poker. The King did not sleep easily, so Minister Martini and I were condemned to staying up with him. We played for symbolic money only, ten Egyptian pounds that the King put into the middle of the table every evening, but at least once a month King Farouk came to visit us and then we played for real money.

King Zog's villa was a hive of diplomatic activity. He made attempts to solve the territorial dispute with Greece through indirect talks with King Paul and he acted as intermediary in quarrels between King Farouk and ex-King Peter of Yugoslavia. He supported the Arabs in their anti-Zionist struggle and was a friend of King Abdullah of Transjordan. The first Western approach to him over the proposed operation was in May 1949, when he received the two American delegates Robert Low and Robert Minor. The meeting went well and he sent a report on it to his friend Jefferson Caffery, US ambassador in Cairo.

On July 7th, immediately after the agreement was settled, McLean flew from Rome to Cairo with Hare and Perkins. A few days later he travelled to Alexandria for the crucial meeting with the King and was joined there by Low and Amery. They had dinner together and the next morning, July 14th, Zog received them at his villa. The King spoke Albanian, Turkish, Arabic, Persian and German very well, but imperfect French and very little English, so the Queen acted as interpreter and Gaqi Gogo kept the record.

The meeting opened disastrously. 'We rather blundered in, proud of having pulled off the Rome agreement, and we imagined that the King would accept what we put to him,' recalls McLean. They said that agreement had been reached between the United States, Britain and a representative group of Albanians abroad to establish a government in exile under Midhat Frasheri's leadership. It was, they seemed to imply, a fait accompli.

The King reacted angrily, rising from his chair and asking the British and American delegates to leave the room. Queen Geraldine remembers his saying, 'It was I who made Albania. I left the country with the Parliament's authority and it is my duty to defend Albania. I cannot pass this duty on to anyone but my heir.' Under whose authority, he asked, had this 'government' been created? By what right had the Americans and British made such decisions and appointments? The delegates departed in disarray.

During the intervening weeks Zog had reconsidered Low's and Minor's proposal. He now believed that it was contrary to his interests to promote a government in exile which he did not lead. He was a skilful politician and he was ready, if his minimal demands were not met, to abort the operation. The delegates therefore conferred and returned to the villa later that day with modified proposals. The King kept them waiting in the villa's main room. All the time they were watched by two large members of the royal guard sitting on a heavy metal chest that contained, Low surmised, the pre-war Bank of Albania's gold reserve. Several tiny cups of Turkish coffee later the King appeared and this time it was Amery who did the talking.

There had been a misunderstanding, Amery explained. The United States and Britain were not establishing a government, only a representative committee, and they were not asking him to give up his royal prerogatives. On the other hand, the time was not yet ripe for the restoration of the Albanian monarchy. The wave of democratic feeling sweeping the world must be taken into account and it would not be possible for Zog to resume the throne before the operation. After the operation had succeeded, of course, it would be a different matter. There could be a national referendum and he could become king again on the basis of the people's will. This was the scheme, said Amery, that Albania's American and British sponsors were ready to back. And it was in Zog's interest to cooperate.

Amery's performance, Low recalls, was masterly: 'I've never seen such diplomacy in my life. He was like Talleyrand. He convinced Zog that he would be best advised "as a firm believer in democracy" to give us his support.' The King's mood became calm and constructive. He spoke kindly, if condescendingly, about Midhat Frasheri, recalling that he had given him a concession to sell books to the Ministry of Education and helped him to make money. He emphasised, though, that 'we need fighters also', implying that in reality Abas Kupi must be recognised, next to himself, as the senior exile figure. He would not support the committee publicly, he said, but he would not oppose it either and he would allow his nominees to take part.

Zog was not informed, of course, that British officers

were already training young Albanians chosen by his republican adversaries, the Balli Kombëtar, and that these were to be the first guerilla fighters to enter Albania under the scheme. On July 17th, after a final and satisfactory morning meeting with the King in Alexandria, the negotiators left for Cairo and the following day flew back to Rome. The diplomatic preliminaries thus successfully concluded, it was time to launch the paramilitary side.

By now the thirty men that Perkins had recruited through Abas Ermenji for the Malta training school were ready to begin work. On the same day that the envoys met King Zog, July 14th, an advance guard consisting of two recruits, Bido Kuka and Sami Lepenica, boarded a British military aircraft near Rome. Two hours later it landed in Malta. They had no documents, very few belongings and they spoke no English. They were told simply that they would be met by a man with a red handkerchief in the top pocket of his jacket.

Alastair Grant, an army captain on secondment to SIS, was on the tarmac ready to greet the two men, but he had no red handkerchief and, as ordered, they walked straight past him. A few yards later they spotted a second SIS officer, Rollo Young, who did have the required handkerchief, so they put themselves in his charge. The immigration officer saluted as the four men walked past. A customs officer wanted to open Kuka's bag. Grant showed him a card that persuaded him not to bother. They got into a car waiting outside and drove for twenty-five minutes through Rabat and up a winding road to Fort Bin Jema in the island's south-west corner.

The fort was part of the Victoria line, a system of defences built in the late nineteenth century to guard against attack from the west. Bin Jema, completed in 1878, was the southernmost of the forts. Its four guns pointed north-west over the steep hill. Its southern and eastern approaches were protected by a deep moat. There was a complicated drawbridge system, known as a chain counterpoise, and a lozenge-shaped keep just outside protected by its own ditch that housed the garrison.

In May David Smiley had returned to London from service with the Royal Horse Guards (the 'Blues') near Hanover to be briefed by Perkins and other SIS officers in Broadway Buildings. In June he flew to Malta, where he spent his first weeks staying at the Xara Palace hotel in Mdina, two miles from the fort. In July his wife Moy joined him with their baby son Xan, just a few weeks old, and her two children Anna and Gavin by a previous marriage. Ron Little, Smiley's batman from the Royal Horse Guards, joined the family and they moved to St Andrew's House, a substantial residence in the north of the island.

Little was Smiley's fifth batman, the other four having been blown up or shot during their boss's various wartime exploits. He had no idea what sort of 'hush hush' business he had volunteered to join and he was mystified when he was interrogated before leaving for Malta in an MI5 office near Marble Arch in London: 'It lasted no more than a few minutes. They asked me whether I was a member of the communist party and that's about all.'

He remembers the secrecy surrounding his aircraft's take-off from an airfield near Cambridge. The sergeant in charge of the flight told him that this was the first time he had escorted a plane load without a passenger list. It was only when he reached the fort that Smiley told him that Albania was the object of the endeavour.

Bill 'Gunner' Collins, Smiley's radio operator from SOE days in Albania, was another member of the team. The two men were close friends, the more so since Collins had saved Smiley's life after a mine exploded under him in Thailand in 1945. Collins installed his equipment in the fort's keep and controlled all communications with SIS in London.

Moy Smiley was the 'cipherene'. She was well trained, having served most of the war as a cipher clerk in the First Aid Nursing Yeomanry (FANY) in Nairobi. It made good security sense to keep the operation 'in the family' as much as possible, to retrain her for a few weeks and put her to work under her husband's command. It saved money too, because she was paid on a temporary basis, there being only two or three hours work for her each day, and she was maintained anyway as an officer's wife without further charge to the taxpayer.

She got up before dawn every morning, drove across the island to the fort and spent two or three hours in a locked room ciphering and deciphering the messages. 'Cipher machines were available at that time, but our operation was small. The message traffic was not fast enough for us to need one,' she says. Instead they used a cipher involving groups of numbers, usually five a line, which were interpreted with special books. Usually a message was 'translated' into cipher letter by letter, though some commonly used words had a five-figure group of their own. The first line of figures indicated the relevant page in the cipher book.

After the work was done she drove back to St Andrew's House, getting home usually by nine o'clock. 'Our aim was to avoid all comment about what we were up to, to keep the image of an ordinary British colonial lifestyle,' she says. 'As a rule in Malta people started work early in the morning and finished by one o'clock or two o'clock, in time for a late lunch, after which there was swimming, riding, tennis, polo and parties. I started even earlier in the morning and I was finished by breakfast-time. This was partly so that I wouldn't be noticed, partly to give me time to run the house as well as do my work.'

The commander-in-chief in Malta, Admiral Sir John Power, gave Smiley the cover of deputy chief of staff in the Castille, Valletta garrison headquarters. Smiley arrived there each morning, knocked on the door of every occupied office, made his presence known to as many people as possible and then half an hour later left for his real day's work at the fort. Inevitably, his almost total absence from his official place of work caused comment among fellow officers, though it was no more than a feeling that he was slacking on the job. They wondered why he was not getting into trouble for his laziness, not whether he was up to something mysterious. He did his best to cultivate this convenient playboy image: 'I used to play polo almost every afternoon, maybe five times a week, giving the impression that I was just a useless cavalry officer doing a not very arduous job.'

Often they went to a party and then, in dinner jacket and long dress, they would call in at the fort for a couple of hours work, deciphering signals, answering them, enciphering answers and leaving them for Collins to send the next morning. Moy Smiley says, 'We led a double life and sometimes we didn't get much sleep.' One evening they were nearly caught out after taking Moy's father to the airport. His flight was cancelled, he returned to St Andrew's House and waited up till the small hours of the night for them to return. Both Moy and David have vivid memories of returning home, finding the old man there unexpectedly and stumbling like naughty children as they tried to think up a story about where they had spent the intervening time.

Very few people in Malta knew Smiley's real occupation. Even the governor, a trade unionist appointed by the Labour government, was kept in the dark. Apart from Admiral Power, the only others who knew that men were being trained in Malta for a secret operation were Captain John Inglis, head of naval intelligence, the MI5 representative Major William Major and Lord Mountbatten, the admiral commanding the First Cruiser Squadron. Later one other person was told, Princess Elizabeth, who came to Malta in November 1949 for the second anniversary of her wedding to Philip, Duke of Edinburgh, then serving in the Royal Navy, as a lieutenant with HMS *Chequers*. They spent two months staying with Mountbatten, Philip's uncle, at Villa Guardamangia in Valletta and were often to be seen with Smiley on or beside the polo field. It was felt that, as heir to the British throne, she was entitled to know about the bizarre plot being hatched in a remote corner of one of her father's colonies.

By far the most notable and colourful officer in Smiley's team was Robert 'Doc' Zaehner, a scholar and linguist, a long-term administrator in the British secret service who later became professor of eastern religions and ethics at Oxford university. Smiley remembers their first meeting when he asked Zaehner, who had just been sent to join him as the operation's interpreter, how good his Albanian was. Zaehner replied, 'I don't speak a word of Albanian, but I do speak classical Persian.'

None of the trainees spoke any Western language, although a few spoke Greek, so the real interpreting was done by two Albanian officers Abdyl Sino and Jani Dilo. (To be fair, it took Zaehner only three months to become fluent in both Albanian and Greek.) Dilo, a law student who spoke French and Italian, instructed the trainees in self-defence and field intelligence. 'I taught them in a classroom with a blackboard two or three hours a day, telling them where to go, whom to meet, what to say, because I know Albania.'

He remembers too, as do all the Albanian survivors, the happy atmosphere of this training period, the relationship between officer and soldier reminiscent of the SOE training schools of Britain in wartime: 'The British gave us very good conditions, treated us like friends, talked to us in off-duty hours, went for walks with us. We were like a family. This means a lot to an Albanian.'

The fort's moat, fifteen feet deep and about as wide, was rigged up as a firing range. The men were trained to climb down a metal ladder screwed into the moat's side by the drawbridge and advance along the angular track, something like a mountain path, firing their submachine-guns at targets springing out of the walls at either side. The moat was also used for grenade-throwing practice and for exploding small charges as part of their training in demolition. Smiley says, 'There was complete security. There was no risk of a shot going wide and killing someone. No one could see us. In fact, it was ideal for the purpose.'

George Odey was a British sergeant in charge of the armoury of light machine-guns and hand-grenades. Alastair Grant taught the Albanians how to use them. There was an intensive programme of physical training, long-distance runs, men carrying weapons and equipment with the officers running beside them equally burdened to set an example. Several times they were taken across the strait to Malta's sister island, Gozo, to practise landing small boats on rocky and sandy shores.

Alfred Howard, a quartermaster major in the Scots Guards and Smiley's deputy, gave lessons in map reading. Smiley passed on his own special knowledge of the use of explosives. Collins taught them how to use the radio and the pedal generator. They lived in the fort, four or five to a room, and did their own cooking. There was a cook for the British soldiers, 'Blondie' Stover, and Corporal John Topliss did the clerical work.

Alan Adams, an eighteen-year-old national serviceman, was a driver in charge of the operation's cars and trucks, having qualified for this sensitive assignment through an eight-week field security course at Maresfield in Sussex. At the end of the course volunteers were invited to enrol for a 'specially sensitive job' in Malta. Adams put his hand up, he recalls, because he liked the aura of mystery surrounding the assignment and because he looked forward to bathing in the Mediterranean.

After a few weeks, though, he became disappointed and disillusioned: 'I thought it was going to be exciting, but in fact all it involved was general duties in the fort and running errands by car or truck around the island. The only thing special about it was that we had to keep our mouths shut.' They were told that lives depended on their discretion and they appreciated this, but Adams was one of many who were disturbed by the informal, lax conditions under which they worked.

He remembers, for instance, Albanian National Day (November 28th) when everyone in the fort, British as well as Albanian, got drunk on ouzo and the young British soldiers took turns throwing grenades into the moat 'just to hear them go off'. Stover the cook drove a fifteen-hundredweight truck over the drawbridge down the winding track, failed to negotiate the sharp right-hand bend and plunged the truck through the wall into a field: 'Everyone just fell about laughing. We were paralytic.'

He feels that such a secret establishment, training men to fight in a hostile land, ought to have been sited in a more secluded spot. As it was, there were shops, bars and cinemas in Mdina, Slima and Rabat, small towns only a few miles away, and the young men from the fort, Albanian as well as British, were allowed to visit them in their off-duty hours without undue restriction, hitch-hiking, walking or cadging a lift in a truck. There was always the risk, it seemed to him, of unguarded talk by the British soldiers and local curiosity was likely to be awakened by the groups of small men wearing British uniform and speaking a language no one could identify.

There were problems too with the military police. The fort's vehicles were unmarked and, since there were no proper maintenance facilities, often dirty or lacking some small part. The MPs used to stop the drivers and ask to see their work sheets. Of course they had no work sheet, just the telephone number of Bill Major's office. The MP had to call the number, whereupon someone in MI5 would tell him to shut up and leave the vehicle alone. The same thing happened when the MPs arrested Albanians in town, never for drunkenness or for the normal soldierly bad behaviour, but for crimes of improper dress, usually for wearing tennis shoes with uniform.

Again and again they would place some mysterious non-English-speaking soldier under lock and key, only to receive a telephone call a few minutes later ordering his release. The MPs became angry. They started complaining and

Major had to explain to them with the full authority of MI5 behind him that there was a special reason why these untidy little men and their badly kept vehicles had to be left alone. He eased the friction further by hosting a drinks party where military police and men from the fort could make friends.

Still, while these arrangements seemed slapdash to some, they seemed no more than the norm to Smiley, Collins and others with experience of SOE and British training methods in subversion and guerilla warfare. This was the technique that had been used a few years earlier in the English country houses where agents were prepared for infiltration into France, Belgium, Norway and Poland. It had worked well then. Why should it not again? It involved placing the utmost trust in the men being trained. It demanded good conditions of work and a family atmosphere.

Smiley was successful in creating these conditions, as all the Albanians involved testify. And it was extremely unlikely that any Albanian would break the rules. After all, they were the ones at risk. Their lives depended on the operation's security. A man does not indulge in loose talk when he knows that in a few weeks' time he will be in enemy territory. Excessive discipline would have been resented by the trainees. It would have seemed like a sign that they were not fully trusted. It would have spoilt the feeling of community and camaraderie that Smiley was trying to foster. The British believed that a brother-to-brother relationship rather than mere friendship was what guerilla fighters needed if they were to give of their best.

In these post-war years British uniform was being worn by men of many nationalities, especially Poles and other displaced persons who served in British pioneer units as they sought to carve out a way of life in a strange country. So it was normal to find British soldiers who were not British by origin and could not speak English. Furthermore, a relaxed attitude to the wearing of uniform was another SOE characteristic from wartime days.

It was the officers who strained local credibility most, especially 'Doc' Zaehner who with his pebble glasses, squeaky voice and 'mad professor' eccentricities was (Smiley recalls) nothing at all like a soldier, let alone an officer, especially since he wore a lieutenant's, captain's or major's uniform as the mood took him.

Jani Dilo and Abdyl Sino wore officers' uniform too. It was felt that this enhanced their authority with the Albanian trainees. It created a problem, though, since Dilo spoke only French, no English at all. The solution was to give Dilo a cover identity as a French-Canadian officer. (The trainees also had cover documents giving them the nationality of any language they spoke, usually Greek or Italian.) One day Dilo was watching a polo match with Smiley when he was introduced to a young woman who turned out to be Princess Elizabeth: 'She was told that I was from Quebec and she explained to me in very good French how to play polo.'

There was only one man at the fort who did not fit in with the 'happy family'. John Papajani, an American of Albanian origin, was assigned to the fort partly as an interpreter, mainly as the United States's symbolic presence. He was appointed because he had worked for Frank Wisner in Cairo during the war, running an OSS luxury villa where agents relaxed between assignments. An American colleague remembers him as an excellent 'fixer' who could provide every possible facility in spite of the rigours of war, something of a 'riverboat gambler'. It was a skill that did not endear him to the team in Malta in 1949, where he is remembered by British and Albanian alike as a large, fat and wild young man, charming but unreliable, not a good choice for a sensitive task.

The Albanians who were at the fort, while they remain critical and even bitter about many aspects of the operation, have no complaint about the training they received and they remember Smiley with particular affection. The period before the first two teams went into Albania at the end of

September was short, no more than ten weeks, but it was enough for them to be taught the basic skills for survival in hostile terrain. It was not expected that they would be put severely to the test in these first forays. They were well armed, they would be in the field only a few weeks and, if there was trouble, they had a clear line of retreat to a friendly country.

In early August Leatham wrote:

> Things are coming along now: accommodation in the fo'c'sle is taking shape, the engine is in for good and one new mast went in on Thursday and looks a very pretty sight. Tomorrow the foremast follows it . . . Our cabins are taking shape and the engine room gets fuller, which all points to an end somewhere. In two weeks from now I hope to be living aboard in the transformed fo'c'sle and Sam and Eileen will follow into the bridal suite aft not long afterwards. Then for the high seas.

By the end of August the Maltese workmen were off the boat and Leatham was living on board. Engine trials and carpentry were completed on September 14th. Barclay was told to make contact with the fort and arrange for the installation of secret equipment. At this point he was instructed, in his view to the point of obsession, to take even more elaborate security precautions.

He left his Valletta hotel, found a public telephone box and called Rollo Young at Fort Bin Jema, using a codeword to identify himself. Young told him to take the bus to Rabat and get off at the sixth milestone. He obeyed and found himself on a deserted stretch of road with one man standing nearby looking the other way. Barclay walked towards him, as instructed, humming a prearranged tune and the man replied with a codeword. Only then could they acknowledge one another and go to the fort. He says, 'We actually did all that, just like they do in the films.'

On September 28th, nine Albanians from the fort were

taken to a nearby cove and put on board a motor fishing vessel, which set off for Otranto, the easternmost point of Italy's heel, only fifty-five miles across the strait from the Albanian coastline. The next day, a Wednesday, Leatham telegraphed his mother, 'Sailing Thursday for Piraeus'. It was less than the full truth. On September 29th the *Stormie Seas* did indeed set sail and their ultimate destination *was* Piraeus; however they were due to make other calls on the way. Their course lay not east to the Greek capital, but north to the same small point on Italy's heel. There, it was arranged, they would meet the 'pixies' and take them into action.

4 The 'little men' go ashore

'Etna loomed large in the west the following morning, though we were at some distance from the coast of Sicily. Soon we made up with the southern shores of Italy and followed the coast for the space of a day before the Gulf of Squillace turned the land away from us and we headed for a familiar point, Capo Santa Maria di Leuca . . .' This is how Leatham recorded the early hours of the *Stormie Seas*'s first active voyage into action. From Santa Maria, the heel's southernmost point, they sailed thirty miles north to Otranto arriving on October 1st.

The 'little men' in the British intelligence 'fishing vessel' were already there. Barclay and Leatham took pains to avoid them on the quayside. The Albanians were pretending to be fishermen of unknown Mediterranean origin, whereas the *Stormie Seas* crew still hoped with the help of Barclay's wife Eileen to pass themselves off as a family boating group. The Italian authorities were not informed of the plan. Leatham did some sightseeing in town and remembers 'the ghastly poverty, the delicious macaroni and the very interesting Norman church with a Tree of Life mosaic floor'.

On October 2nd at midday the 'fishing boat' put out to sea and an hour later the *Stormie Seas* followed. They had arranged to meet at a rendezvous point twenty miles to the east. At this point, well out of sight of land, they broke their cover. A rubber boat was lowered and the nine 'little men' were rowed across to the *Stormie Seas* with all their equipment: German Schmeiser submachine-guns, ammunition, food, water, medical supplies, propaganda leaflets and photographs of the émigré leaders. They had Albanian money too, but their main currency was the gold sovereign. Each man had a 'reserve' of fifty coins which he carried in a small sack attached to his waist.

The sea transfer was their first mistake. Although out of sight of land, they could be seen from the top of Otranto lighthouse, which is tall enough to lengthen the horizon to twenty-two miles. It later emerged that Italian intelligence agents were well aware of what the British were doing and they made use of this vantage point to watch the entire transfer through telescopes. They did not protest or interfere, but they passed the information on to the CIA in Washington, with whom their relationships were particularly close.

Barclay and Leatham hoped to land their men that evening, but a severe electric storm blew up and their radio equipment was damaged by lightning. It was impossible to continue, because Geoffrey Kelly the radio operator was due to report the landing as soon as it happened. And some of the young Albanians were so seasick that they could not go into action. They therefore altered course slightly southwards and made for somewhere to lay up quietly at anchor, choosing the small Greek island of Othoni, twenty-five miles north-west of Corfu.

By the morning of October 3rd the radio was working again. Then there was another nasty moment when a Greek customs vessel approached. It was no more than a friendly visit, but if the officers had come on board there would have been no way of explaining away nine armed men and a cabin full of strange equipment. Eileen was ordered to charm them away with cigarettes, ouzo and sweet talk.

Barclay recalls, 'After offering them cigarettes, she found that she hadn't got any. She was fumbling for a packet, asking John and me where they were, when a hand appeared up out of the engine room, belonging to someone who wasn't supposed to be there at all, and gave her a packet.' Leatham admits to being 'very scared' at this point. It was a frontier area and Greece was in a state of civil war, with communist rebels using Albania as a safe haven. And the Albanian coast was only twenty miles away.

They eventually left Othoni that afternoon reaching their objective, Albania's Karaburun peninsula, at about nine o'clock. They stopped engines half a mile from shore, out of rifle range, and pulled up the dory that they were towing, a surf boat like a large Scandinavian pram with a sawn-off transom bow. Derby and Lofty got into the dinghy, helped the nine 'pixies' down into it with their equipment and rowed for the line of cliffs that loomed above them through the moonless night. They made hardly a sound, but Mavros the boatman had to keep the engine idling to stop the *Stormie Seas* drifting away and its quiet rumble echoed across the water alarmingly.

It was 'Seaview', the exact spot where Smiley and McLean had swum for their lives at the end of 1943. Smiley's memories of the place were vivid and, after inspecting aerial photographs to make sure that its main features remained unchanged, he had explained every detail of it to his Malta trainees. The same goat tracks were there, leading over the mountains and into the interior.

Derby and Lofty edged the boat between the inlet's jaws, took their boots off and leapt ashore, pulling the boat close in so that the men could climb on to the rocks and keep their feet dry for the night's march. They would have to climb the steep ridge and be well away from the beach before dawn. Derby took the infra-red signal lamp, whose light can be seen only through special glasses, and flashed a message to the *Stormie Seas* indicating that all was well. The two marines rowed back there on their own.

The nine men set off up the track. At the outset they felt safe on the mountainous, uncultivated and almost uninhabited Karaburun ridge. They followed certain simple rules, avoiding easy tracks and keeping away from water sources which are well-known ambush points for unwary Albanian travellers. They marched mostly at night, hiding in caves during the day. They stayed together as far as Mount Tragjas, ten miles east of the landing place, but the going was so hard that it took them forty-eight hours to get there.

They then divided into two groups. Bido Kuka and four others made for Kurvelesh, their home region not far from the Greek border. The other four, including the Lepenica cousins Hysen and Sami, went north towards Valona. At this point of separation, Kuka remembers, they had a definite feeling of the tragedy that was to come. They just knew, he says, that the communists were ready waiting for them.

As soon as they reached the village of Gjorm they heard the bad news. The Lepenica group had been ambushed a few hours after striking out northwards. The two cousins were killed and so was a third man, Zogoll Sheno. The fourth man disappeared. They were told this by a young girl who ran out to meet them as they approached the village shouting, 'Brothers, you're all going to be killed.' She told them not only about the attack on the Lepenica group, but also that a few days earlier the Albanian army chief of staff Beqir Balluku had brought in his forces and surrounded the whole coastal area. They knew then that their fears were well founded. They decided to lie low. The girl gave them some bread and milk and they hid in caves outside the village.

The Albanian government, it appears, were not taken by surprise. They were well aware, if not of precise dates and landing places, certainly of the operation's general timing and location. Villages were alerted and the security forces had ordered everyone, especially shepherds on the hillsides who were likely to see travellers on foot, to report anything suspicious. It was only a few days since Kim Philby had been briefed about the operation before leaving for New

York. Everything he learnt from British intelligence about the proposed operation had been communicated to the Soviet secret service and the Albanian police before he embarked on the S.S. *Caronia*.

It is also the view of James J. Angleton, the CIA officer who monitored the operation's security, that information about it leaked to the Soviet side from the many émigrés living in the West, particularly in Rome, who were involved in its planning and recruitment. Western intelligence men assume that émigrés are a prime target of Soviet intelligence, since they have made themselves into a threat by the very act of escaping from Soviet control. They believe that since 1917 almost every important anti-communist émigré group has been successfully infiltrated by the KGB and its predecessors. It began, they say, with Feliks Dzierżyński and the 'Trust'. And it continues today.

On Corfu, just a few dozen miles away, there was a British intelligence radio base commanded by Alan Hare. SIS had taken over the Villa Bimbelli, known as 'The Palace', a large mansion in the north-east of the island perched on a hill overlooking the Corfu channel and the Albanian coast. A team of radio technicians and coders helped by Jani Dilo and Abdyl Sino as translators spent October there waiting for the guerilla fighters to come on the air and report progress.

Every day they listened in at a prearranged hour, but time passed and nothing was heard. Then around October 12th Ahmet Kuka, Bido's cousin, came on the air with a quick message from the group's hiding place near Gjorm. Dilo says, 'I was the first one to make contact with the boys. They told us that things had gone wrong, that three men had been killed and that the police knew everything about them. It was terrible and they were so scared.'

The code-system they used was rudimentary. There had been no time to train the operators in morse. They used plain speech and each group had a book in which places, names and simple actions were designated by a number. It was not secure, since even without the code-book a large part of the signal could be understood by anyone who happened to overhear.

The radio itself was a constant problem. The pedal generator was essential, since they could never count on finding suitable batteries, but it weighed twenty kilograms, as much as the radio itself, and the slightest knock made it stiff and hard to operate. Sino remembers seeing the radio equipment and being shocked by its bulkiness. It was the right sort of radio for an infantry platoon, he thought, not for a guerilla unit. Most dangerous of all was the loud whining noise when the generator was pedalled at the correct speed.

Every time a group sent a message they had to abandon their hiding place, leaving a man to guard the equipment, and look for a transmitting point. Usually they looked for a stream in the hope that the noise of running water would drown the generator's whine. However, if they were near a stream, there would be hills between them and the Corfu listening point, so sometimes they transmitted from higher ground in order to improve reception. The man on the pedals had to work hard to make the necessary electricity, and to make matters worse the generator was susceptible to the slightest knock. Pedalling became even harder and the noise terrifyingly loud as it echoed across the valley and risked raising the alarm.

Kuka's group left Gjorm and took four days to cover the twenty-five miles to Nivica, their home town in the Kurvelesh area, where they spent a week resting and collecting food. They were known and trusted in the area, so they found many sympathisers. They gave out their leaflets and photographs, explained the need to build cells of opposition and discussed possible sabotage targets.

They could not be sure, though, how far the warm welcome they received indicated willingness to join their struggle. It would have been unthinkable for the Nivica villagers not to welcome and feed such a group. They were known in the village and anyway the laws of hospitality ensured a generous reception for all travellers. However, the same laws absolve a host of all responsibility once the travellers have left the vicinity of his home. A householder might receive a group even though he did not agree with their mission, then kill or denounce them the following day. They made a rule therefore never to spend a night under a villager's roof. They accepted food, but turned down all offers of a bed, however tempting.

They told friends, family and others whom they trusted that the time was ripe to remove the hated Hoxha regime, that the United States and Britain were committed to this goal and had promised to help them. They wanted the local people to form resistance groups, in which case they would leave them gold, money (Albanian leks) and the radio. They would then retreat through Greece and return with more men, money and equipment. British aircraft would drop them supplies, as they had five years earlier.

A centre of anti-communism financed by Britain and the United States would gradually be built up not only in Nivica, Kuka and his friends explained, but also in dozens of other Albanian towns and villages. They had the necessary back-up, a training base in Malta, a communications base in Corfu, the potential for a serious resistance organisation. At the right moment they would all strike, eliminate the communists and create democratic government.

The Albanian villagers took a more complicated view. Although many were eager in principle to fight against the communists, they were unimpressed by the arrival of only five guerilla fighters, simple tribesmen without even an officer in command. They were sceptical. 'Why are there only five of you?' they asked the Kuka group. 'Why have you not brought us arms?' They remembered the anti-fascist battle five years earlier when the British sent in trained agents including British officers and dropped them supplies by parachute from the SOE bases in Cairo and Bari in southern Italy. What was happening now was feeble by comparison.

Still, the reaction was not entirely negative. They were interested in what the group had to say; they did not like the Hoxha government and they wanted it to disappear. They were cautious only because they were doubtful about the present plan. If there were a real sign of Western commitment to Hoxha's removal, then they would begin to take the plan seriously. Towards the end of October the Kuka cousins and their three friends decided to retreat into Greece and report this feeling.

Ahmet Kuka and Turhan Aliko went by one route, Bido Kuka, Hysen Isufi and Ramis Matuka by another. The border was only thirty-five miles away as the crow flies but the mountains and communist patrols made it a long and arduous march. Ahmet Kuka and Aliko reached Greece without serious incident, but the other three had four encounters with communist forces.

Bido Kuka remembers the night when they were challenged while walking in file along a ravine: 'They told us to identify ourselves. We shouted back, "Who are you?" When they said they were police we opened fire, but they were in defended positions and we didn't make much impression. Matuka was hit by a bullet and killed instantly. Then Isufi and I retreated. Eventually we got to Greece.' Of the nine men who took part in the first landing four had been killed, one disappeared and four made it back to safety.

Meanwhile Barclay and Leatham had sailed back towards Italy and collected another group of young Albanians who were transferred to their boat on the high seas. This time there were eleven of them, five from the Korçë area and six from Gjirokaster. On October 10th they were landed in the same way as before on a sandy beach north of Valona and they set out for their home areas.

Sefer Muço, leader of the Korçë group, got his men to their destination safely, then began distributing émigré newspapers and pamphlets, receiving the same cautious reaction. The local people were pleased to see him, he recalls, and promised to pass the material on, but they were sceptical about the plan's chances of success. Muço told them, as he had been led to believe, that very soon it would become clear that the Western allies were determined to overthrow communist power. For the moment they were keeping a low profile, but soon they would declare themselves.

Neither he nor they knew that this involved an internal contradiction in the operation's planning. It would never be possible for the United States and Britain to 'declare themselves' for Hoxha's overthrow. The whole enterprise had to be kept secret, since it was being done without the people's knowledge. It did not even have the basis of a Cabinet decision. President Truman and Prime Minister Attlee had been informed about it, but had given verbal agreement only. The details had been entrusted to a very small group of professionals.

It had been a condition of giving the go-ahead that the two intelligence services must hide every sign of American or British involvement. They must maintain 'capacity for plausible denial'. This restricted what they could do for their young Albanian agents. If any new piece of British military hardware or, worse still, any British officer were captured by the communists, they would be paraded before the world as proof of the West's aggression. This could never be allowed to happen.

This was not the Second World War, when it was quite normal to send guerillas or commandos to attack the enemy. The United States and Britain were at peace with the world, even with Albania, although they had no diplomatic links with her, and the armed attack that they had sponsored was a clear violation of international law. This took the issue far wider than Albania. It involved basic attitudes of Western diplomacy, in particular relations with the Soviet Union, Albania's protector, and many other countries including Yugoslavia, Italy and Greece.

The incident of the Greek customs men at Othoni, near Corfu, was an example of this danger. There would have been a scandal if Greek officials had come aboard *Stormie Seas* and found illegal men and equipment. True, a few senior Greek officers such as army chief Alexander Papagos and his commando general Fouli Kalinski knew about the British plan and had given approval. It would not have taken British intelligence long to get Barclay, Leatham and the others out of jail. But by then great damage would have been done. Word would go out that the British were up to 'funny business' off the Albanian coast. From then on Leatham and Barclay would be marked men and the *Stormie Seas* a marked boat. The Greek government would be seriously embarrassed. It would have meant the end of their association with the 'firm' and perhaps of the whole operation.

An even more dangerous event took place after the October 10th landing near Valona. Barclay and Leatham knew that they must be out of Albanian waters by daybreak, but a sirocco, a strong wind from the south-east, blew up an hour or two after the landing and they could make no headway towards Greece or Italy. The force of the gale cut loose the dory used to land the men. Their only hope was to seek shelter. Leatham says, 'It really was a classic case of "any port in a storm", even if it meant the enemy port.'

Hugging the Albanian coast, they struggled a few miles south and, leaving Saseno Island on their right, entered the Gulf of Valona. 'It is amazing that we weren't spotted,' says Leatham. 'We knew there was a Russian submarine base on the island and we could see the lights of Valona as we clawed our way past it.' They anchored in the shelter of the Gulf, hoping that the storm would abate before dawn and give them time to escape in the darkness.

At dawn the sirocco was still blowing and they were alarmed to see soldiers taking up positions on the beach a hundred yards away. Then the soldiers began pointing rifles at them, gesticulating to them to come ashore and explain themselves. Barclay and Leatham had no intention of complying. The Albanians were unlikely to believe their cover story, in spite of the young woman in their midst. The six young men still on board, five British and one Greek, had a distinctly warlike look about them and any search of the boat would have yielded a mass of incriminating evidence. They decided instead to rely on the notoriously poor seamanship of the Albanian nation and make a run for it.

Seeing that the Englishmen were not going to obey their gestures, the soldiers opened fire. Leatham says, 'As soon as we heard the shots, we slipped the anchor and ran back to sea as fast as we could. The weather had calmed down a little, so we extricated ourselves from the Gulf of Valona, slightly peppered, minus one anchor and one dory but otherwise intact.' The soldiers fired flares to alert the garrison on Saseno and as they squeezed past the island the Englishmen thought they might be chased by a patrol boat, but a strong gale was still blowing and either the flares were not seen or the garrison felt disinclined to put to sea.

The *Stormie Seas* fought her way through the sirocco down to Corfu. 'Arrived Corfu today sailing Piraeus Saturday [the 15th],' cabled Leatham to his mother on October 13th. The next day he wrote to her in Homeric terms describing the gales and the sunrise over the Albanian hills that 'pouring light towards the northern Ionian islands like molten metal out of a ladle'. He did not explain why he was there or why it had taken them two weeks to sail from Malta to Corfu.

By the end of October it was snowing in Albania's Korçë area. Life in the caves was hard for Sefer Muço and his four friends. They took food from the villagers, but never felt able to trust them enough to spend nights in the warmth of their homes. 'In every family there is always one who is a communist or afraid of the communists,' says Muço. His proud boast is that he was a cautious and mistrustful guerilla fighter, so cautious that he never lost a man.

Bardhyl Gerveshi, a member of the Gjirokaster group, remembers long nights on the march and days when they rested, eating the dehydrated food given them by the British. If there was no stream, they gathered water by hanging out groundsheets before dawn and collecting any dew or rainwater that trickled down into tins. They never started a march before darkness was complete and they planned each route so as to arrive at a suitable hiding place by five o'clock every morning. This gave them an hour to get comfortable in the wood or cave before daybreak. They spent the days sleeping and planning the next march, taking turns to mount guard.

They had maps, but not good enough maps to show a safe route from Valona to Gjirokaster. Maps with the detail they required simply did not exist and they preferred to rely on photographs taken from the air. These showed individual pathways, they recall, even individual rocks. Most important of all, though, was the local knowledge of group members. The team was comprised so that at each stage of the route there was always someone who knew the way through to the next point.

They were travelling in traditional Albanian fashion. Travel on foot made sense in such a small country, with hardly any railway or roads, consisting of valleys linked by steep mountain paths, too steep for vehicles, passable only on foot or by mule. It was an efficient method and four or five was the ideal group number. A lone traveller was likely to be robbed and killed. A group of twenty would cause alarm. The arrival of so many strangers meant an imminent attack on the village or settlement. The British knew about this through their wartime experiences, which they were trying to copy.

However, in other ways their behaviour was not traditional. It was unusual for men to travel at night instead of making use of the hospitality rules, which gave shelter and protection until the next day and as far as the village limits. Smiley says, 'If you entered an Albanian house, the owner would take your rifle off your shoulder and hang it up and from that moment your life was in that man's hands. If you were killed while you were that man's guest, he would mount a feud against the whole family of the man who had killed you. And it would go on until someone had been killed in revenge.'

Every night's march was a complicated matter. They could never walk through a village, even when everyone was asleep. The dogs would be awake and their barking would rouse everyone in the vicinity. This is how Albanian villagers protect themselves. They had to find the right mountain path through to the next valley, always in darkness, and make a detour whenever they came near a village, at the same time keeping an eye out for police patrols, checking that they were moving in the right direction and making sure that there was enough darkness left for them to find a hiding place. If they were ever caught by the dawn in a stretch of open country, they were bound to be spotted and arrested or killed.

Gerveshi says:

> The woods were the best. They gave us good cover, it was not too cold, you could sometimes find water, even something to eat. We had to make sure we were deep inside the trees, otherwise we could be caught by villagers who brought their goats in. Otherwise we looked for a cave, one with big stones to cover the entrance, not too near the valley, because then there would be people about during the day, and not too high up because of the cold.
>
> Before choosing a cave we always checked the area nearby for goat or sheep droppings. If there were, it meant that in a couple of hours the place would be surrounded by animals and shepherds. We were never cold during the night because we had warm clothes and

> we were always on the move, but we were sometimes cold during the day, especially since there was no question of lighting a fire. We tried to choose caves that faced east, so that the sun warmed it up after a cold night.

Their worst moment, Gerveshi remembers, was when they ventured out of a cave in daylight, thinking that no one was about, to plan the night's march. Suddenly they saw some shepherds walking towards them. What were they to do? They thought of running away, but this would look very suspicious and the men might easily report them to the police. They thought of killing them and were deterred only by the thought that this would start a blood feud.

Albanian families are large. They include cousins as well as brothers. Therefore, if they killed three shepherds, they might find themselves with a hundred angry relatives on their trail, all duty-bound to exact revenge. The relatives would be more dangerous than the police. So they decided to bluff the situation out. Gerveshi says, 'We covered up the guns and hand-grenades with our jackets. When they got close, we told them that we were surveyors mapping the region. Our leader Haki Gaba asked them for a cigarette and they gave him one. We joked our way through it.'

They reached the Gjirokaster area and began making contact with friends and family. They even ventured into villages, armed only with pistols, having left the heavy equipment under guard in a hiding place. They made contact with Corfu briefly, but their recruiting efforts were not successful and there was little to report. Then the generator broke down. The man on the pedals found it impossible to work fast enough to make the necessary electricity. The machinery was too stiff, either through lack of oil or because it had been dropped or jolted. The radio was useless without the generator, so they left it with a relative, Haki Gaba's cousin, and made for the Greek border hoping to return with a replacement. The border is only thirteen miles from

Gjirokaster. Gerveshi knew the area intimately and they crossed into Greece safely.

In Corfu Abdyl Sino and Jani Dilo found themselves being driven crazy by the anxiety and the waiting. They were joined by Ihsan Toptani, a multilingual Albanian aristocrat educated in Austria and well known to British agents from wartime days. They went swimming and boating together. Every few days Alan Hare took them into town in his big Humber station wagon. The Albanian shore was only five miles across the strait from the villa and they spent hours looking longingly at it through binoculars.

Every evening they tuned in hoping for news from 'the boys'. But the messages were rare and often indistinct, in spite of the short distance. Hills got in the way of the signal and the whine of the generator was so loud that the words and coded numbers could hardly be heard. They decided that all groups must in future use the Morse code, that the men must be better trained and the radio equipment modernised.

Sefer Muço's men decided to move their hiding place down the mountain because of the snow. They were bothered by the cold and by fears that the tracks they made by the cave's entrance would be spotted by the authorities. Once they moved down below the snowline, however, they were in danger of being found by farmers or shepherds. But their radio was working and one evening they heard Dilo telling them, 'You will proceed at once to sixty-four.' Muço went for his code-book and found that 'sixty-four' meant 'Greece'. He has a vivid memory of the snow falling outside the cave and his boys inside jumping up and down with happiness shouting, 'Sixty-four! Sixty-four!'

Gerveshi and Haki Gaba went back into Albania with a replacement generator and contacted Gaba's brother Betas. The news was bad. The cousin they had left the radio with was under arrest. He had approached a friend and tried to recruit him to fight the communists. The man had promptly denounced him to the police. Betas explained that no one in the area wanted to get involved in anti-communist action on so small a scale. He had tried several possible recruits. All had given the same reply. And it was only a matter of a few days, he thought, before he too was arrested.

They therefore took Betas Gaba with them when they withdrew to Greece again a few days later. Gerveshi says, 'It was impossible. The communists had too tight a grip. They were too well organised.' They later learnt from British officers in Greece that the cousin had been tortured and executed, though not before he had given the police the British radio together with the relevant codewords and full details on how he came to be recruited.

The result of the first two landings was therefore unsuccessful. Four of the twenty men put ashore were lost and the others had failed to inspire any genesis of an anti-government movement. Several Albanian civilians had also been arrested and killed. The planners in American and British intelligence felt, nevertheless, that the results, though disappointing, were not disastrous.

They had hoped for more success in the recruitment of agents, but they were not unduly surprised by the failure. Recruitment would start when the young men were better trained and more politically aware. The operation was still in its early stages. More groups would be sent in 1950 and the word would get about that the West was serious in its determination. It was clear from these first reports that Hoxha's regime was deeply unpopular. The West needed only to make a show of strength and rebellion would begin in earnest.

The 20 per cent loss of agents was by wartime standards not unusual. The survivors had shown that the operation's basis was apparently sound. It was possible for small groups to move about the Albanian mountains in traditional fashion, as British officers had observed during the war. The men needed more training, especially in the use of radio. The mistakes made by the first groups would be analysed and taken into account for the benefit of future landings. It would be wrong to abandon such an important enterprise, the result of immense tactical and political groundwork, simply because there was nothing much to show from the first few days in the field. They must persevere, it was felt, and maintain the pressure on Stalin's weak and isolated ally.

5 Philby in Washington

The SS *Caronia* with Kim Philby on board reached New York on October 8th, 1949, five days after the first landing of young Albanians at 'Seaview'. On October 10th British ambassador Oliver Franks advised the State Department that Philby had joined his team in Washington as a 'first secretary'. He lived with his wife Aileen and their children in a large frame house in a fashionable Washington district, 5228 Nebraska Avenue, and soon established himself as one of the American capital's wittiest and most entertaining hosts. He was generous in his hospitality towards colleagues from England also. He writes, 'The more visitors I had in Washington, the more spies I got my finger into. That, after all, was my aim in life.'[29]

His real job was that of British intelligence representative in the United States, responsible for links both with the Federal Bureau of Investigation under J. Edgar Hoover and with the Central Intelligence Agency under Admiral Roscoe Hillenkoetter. His main contact in the CIA was a driving force in the intelligence gathering Office of Strategic Operations, James J. Angleton, and the two men lunched together every week at Harvey's restaurant. They became friendly, Philby writes, though both had ulterior motives, bearing in mind the national rivalry of the profession: 'By cultivating me to the full, he could better keep me under wraps. For my part, I was more than content to string him along. The greater the trust between us overtly, the less he would suspect covert action.'[30]

He was also SIS's link with the Office for Policy

Coordination (OPC), set up in June 1948 to carry out anti-Soviet covert operations. A National Security Council (NSC) directive, referring to the 'vicious covert activities' of the Soviet Union and her allies, authorised a discreet campaign of propaganda, sabotage, subversion, economic warfare and assistance to underground resistance groups. The condition was that all such activity be 'so planned and conducted that any US government responsibility for them is not evident to unauthorised persons and that if uncovered the US government can plausibly disclaim any responsibility for them'.[31]

OPC's structure was unusual. Although it received money from CIA, its director was responsible not to them but to the NSC and the State Department's policy planning staff, headed by George Kennan. In September 1948 secretary of state George Marshall appointed Frank Wisner, a former lawyer and OSS Balkan specialist, as OPC's first director. During its four years of existence it was this body, not CIA, that was responsible for American secret subversive operations abroad.

OPC's small staff worked in the Lincoln Building near the Washington reflecting pool and it was they who received the go-ahead in March 1949 to launch the American side of the Albanian operation. Frank Lindsay was Wisner's deputy in charge of eastern Europe and Jim McCargar, another OSS veteran and the author of several books on espionage under the name 'Christopher Felix', was responsible for south-east Europe. As such McCargar was appointed as the Albanian plan's 'commander'. The 'special policy committee' that ran the operation on a day-to-day basis also included representatives of the two foreign services, Robert Joyce of the State Department and George, 2nd Earl Jellicoe, another first secretary at the British embassy, since he was the officer in the embassy responsible for Balkan affairs. McCargar's British opposite number and joint commander of Albanian plans was, of course, Kim Philby.

McCargar recalls that Philby came to Washington with a

great reputation, especially among Americans who had heard about him and looked forward to his arrival. He had just emerged from an internal SIS quarrel in which he massacred his adversaries, led by his former departmental chief Felix Cowgill. He seemed to be a master of intrigue, the leader of the 'young Turks' in British intelligence, a man likely in due course to become director of the entire service.

His drinking was always phenomenal, but unlike his fellow traitor Donald Maclean he did not behave scandalously while under the influence. And he owed his survival to the fact that he was never indiscreet. A British security officer who helped towards his eventual unmasking remembers him as quiet, determined, the sort of Englishman that Americans like. He had a stammer that he seemed to cultivate, since it helped with the timing of his repartee, and he avoided politics even when drunk. All this was seen and noted by his British superiors. It commended him to them, since it enhanced his cover as a spy. And at the same time it enabled him to deceive them.

Pat Whinney, with whom Philby stayed in Athens on his way home from Istanbul in mid-1949, is one of the few colleagues who disliked him personally:

> Maria and I had to go out. We left him with dinner and the whisky decanter, all of which he drank. He was so sure of himself, so sure that he was right. He would not warm to you unless you were prepared to flatter him, which I was not, or to match him quip for quip, which I was not prepared to do because I knew he'd beat me. He was rather like Malcolm Muggeridge, caustic and sarcastic, full of intellectual arrogance.

This was not the impression that he gave in Washington. Robert Low recalls, 'He entertained a lot of Americans. The wine flowed and the whisky too. He had a stammer and a good stock of anecdotes – an excellent combination.'

McCargar says, 'He had charm, warmth and an engaging, self-deprecating humour. He drank a lot, but then so did we all in those days. We floated out of the war on a sea of drink without its having much effect. I considered him a friend. In other words, I was completely taken in.'

He remembers Philby coming to him soon after arriving with important news about the first Albanian landings. The same piece of news reached McCargar through American channels a week later. It was, the two commanders agreed, an illustration of Britain's excellent code and communication system. Philby thereupon, with a look of complete innocence, offered to put his facilities at McCargar's disposal for any American messages that concerned the operation. Even for McCargar, who at that stage trusted Philby completely, this was too much. 'I told him, very politely, no.'

Another American closely involved in the operation remembers meeting Philby in Perkins's Broadway office and dining with him that evening at a well-known London fish restaurant. They discussed the Albanian operation. Philby had been presented to him, he explains, in circumstances that made him a trusted ally, one of the inner circle, so he had no reason to hold back in any discussion of their joint enterprise. He noticed Philby's drinking and his stammer, but recalls that the latter made him feel sympathy for the man more than anything. Even today he is horrified at the thought that he spent an entire evening discussing a secret operation, one in which lives were being put at risk, with a Soviet agent.

George Jellicoe, son of the famous British admiral and victor of the Battle of Jutland, had joined the Foreign Office after a gallant war spent fighting with the Greek resistance. He too was completely deceived by Philby: 'I liked Kim very much – and his wife Aileen. I remember them coming to Patsy's and my house in Waterside Drive quite often. I found him convivial, the same word that he uses about me in his book.'

He remembers frequent meetings with Philby in the SIS offices at the Washington embassy. They would sit together reading the telegrams about the operation's progress, most of them from SIS headquarters but a few of them from the Foreign Office: 'Kim was the one who made all the operational decisions. I was just there to give political guidance, from the diplomatic point of view. He was intelligent, professional and hard working. How on earth he found the time to do a job for the Russians as well as for us I just don't know.'

The two commanders, Philby and McCargar, were given an office in the Pentagon building where they could discuss the operation and meet their men from the field, Robert Low for instance, without attracting attention by bringing them to OPC headquarters. In the event it was not often used, since most of their talks took place in private homes or in the open, but McCargar remembers that OPC felt it important to keep the room, even though it was locked almost all the time, as a piece of window-dressing and a demonstration in the eyes of the military of the young organisation's status.

It was here that a *post mortem* was held on the landings from the *Stormie Seas*. It was noted that four of the twenty Albanian agents had been lost, that no acts of sabotage had been carried out and that attempts to recruit inside the country had failed. What worried London and Washington most of all was the evidence provided during debriefing in Greece that the Albanian authorities knew about the landings in advance and had taken special precautions at precisely the right time, early October, to deal with infiltrators. The disappearance of the Lepenica group south of Valona was particularly disturbing, as was the fact that Albanian army chief of staff Beqir Balluku had mobilised his men to comb the countryside near Karaburun.

Robert Low, who was now back in Washington after his Rome negotiations, says, 'It was obvious that there was a leak somewhere. The communists just knew too much about these people we were sending in. We had several meetings, trying to figure out where the thing was going wrong, whether there might be a leak in Malta or Rome. The Albanians weren't happy about it either. So we had to ask ourselves how long we could go on dropping these young men into the bag.'

They had no idea, of course, that Philby had told what he knew about the forthcoming landings to his Soviet contact in London in late September, that the whole plan was therefore, as he observes in his book, futile from the beginning. Low says, 'I realise now that I was playing poker with a mirror behind my head.'

Philby describes the Albanian operation prominently in his book, padding it out with references to alleged British prejudice and personal remarks about others who took part. He records Wisner as 'running self-importantly to fat', Albanian leaders Hasan Dosti as 'a young weakling' and Abas Kupi as 'an old rascal', Jellicoe, Joyce and Lindsay as 'convivial souls'. He observes that the Albanian agents 'nowhere found arms open to welcome them', but the part he himself played in ensuring the operation's failure is something he leaves to the reader's assumption.

Philby's treachery was not, however, the operation's only security lapse. There were, it is assumed by Western intelligence, leaks from among the Albanian community in Rome, where the Albanian embassy was very active, and from Athens too. This problem was made worse by the operation's reliance on Second World War experience. Wartime communication between countries was banned, restricted or censored. But now the world was at peace. People travelled freely and communicated by mail, cable or telephone. McCargar says, 'This was not the Mediterranean of 1942–3. It was the Mediterranean of 1949, which was open and leaking like a sieve.'

There was also the Italian dimension. Rome was the Albanian émigré centre and there was a large Albanian community in Sicily. The exiles had no money, employment or documents. They were beholden to Italy for every kind of favour and the Italian authorities were in an ideal position to put pressure on them.

Even as a defeated nation Italy retained her interest in Albania. Here in an area of traditional Italian influence, she resented the way in which the United States and Britain used her territory as a base for subversive operations, without seeking permission. Her intelligence service employed Albanian exiles, mostly Catholics from the Independenza party who had been trained in Italy between the wars and served Italy during the 1939–43 occupation. At the same time Italy's communist party was especially strong. In April 1948 there was a traumatic general election in which the communist/socialist alliance ran the Christian Democrats a close second.

James Angleton, whose links with the Italian services were close, confirms what Leatham and Barclay suspected when they left Otranto on October 2nd, 1949, that they were observed by Italian agents with telescopes from the top of the nearby lighthouse. He remembers 'the flurry of telegrams' from his Italian friends that followed this 'secret' departure from an Italian port. And McCargar recalls Angleton telephoning him that day 'with great glee' to invite him to his office. He then described to McCargar the precise circumstances under which the *Stormie Seas* had left Otranto, advising him that as far as the Italians were concerned the Albanian operation was well and truly blown.

The relationship between CIA, represented by Angleton, and the OPC 'subversives' was one of healthy rivalry. Angleton seemed to be saying that if he knew so much others must know more, so OPC would be best advised to pull itself together and tighten security. McCargar says, 'His motive was ostensibly to warn me as a colleague, but I imagine that he was also anxious to show off his own omniscience to us OPC newcomers.'

Such information might be sold for money. It might be leaked for reasons of resentment against the United States and Britain who had usurped Italy's Albanian role. Or it might be passed on for reasons of ideological principle. There were many Italians, not only communists but those of liberal views also, who detested the idea of some new Albanian venture. It smacked to them of the expansionist policies of the fascist era, policies that had brought Italy to disaster. It would seem to them normal to enlist the help of a communist embassy in order to defeat any such plan.

There were even some journalists who had an inkling of what was taking place, even though what they wrote seems not to have been taken seriously by the public. 'The Albanian volcano is ready to explode,' reported the London *News Chronicle* on September 14th, 1949. Cyrus L. Sulzberger, the *New York Times*'s influential correspondent in the Mediterranean sent a series of dispatches about the operation, details of which he picked up from embassy contacts during his Balkan travels. First he wrote that 'the weakening and eventual changing of the Albanian regime' was a Western 'basic objective'. Then he reported stronger anti-communist resistance in Albania and increased recruitment to the guerilla bands. Then he came up with a report which, although brief, was specific and alarmingly accurate. Two groups had been landed on the Albanian coast, he wrote, with orders to take radios into the hinterland and build up communications with the anti-Hoxha movement.[32]

McCargar was furious when he read Sulzberger's last report. It was an irresponsible and unpatriotic act, he told him at the first opportunity. Sulzberger's riposte was that his report was based on what he had heard from several of his Mediterranean contacts, including an American diplomat who had discussed it over lunch, and that McCargar should take this fact as measure of the operation's security as a whole. Sulzberger remembers how telegrams seemed to fly to Belgrade, Rome and Athens whenever he mentioned Albania: 'Several government officials mentioned it to me, quite angrily, and asked me what my source was. I told them it was none of their business. I can't think why they were so upset. There seemed to be plenty of people in the Balkans who knew what was happening and obviously the Russians knew about it down to the last semi-colon.'

Efforts were therefore put under way to salvage what was left of the operation's secrecy. At the same time, though, the political side was given as much publicity as possible. Albanians would help the guerillas only if they knew which leaders the guerillas represented. The 'off the peg' Albanian government so carefully put together by Low, Amery, McLean and Hare during June/July 1949 was the essential basis of everything that the guerillas hoped to achieve, a group of men offered to the Albanian people as an alternative to the communists presently ruling them. Obviously this offer had to be made publicly, the more publicly the better.

Therefore at the end of August 1949, while Abas Ermenji was in Malta, staying with the Smiley family in St Andrew's House and giving morale-boosting lectures on Albanian history to the men about to depart on their mission, the other émigré leaders were on their way to the main Western capitals to advertise their existence and their cause. On August 26th Frasheri, Kupi, Kryeziu, Nuçi Kota and Zef Pali gave a press conference in Paris announcing the formation of the Albanian National Committee. They represented, they said, 'all those Albanians who wish to establish a democratic government and fundamental human liberty' and they pledged themselves 'to guide and encourage our brave people in their resistance to cruel communist tyranny'. Nothing was said, of course, about what Ermenji was doing in Malta or about the existence of a military dimension.

They then flew to London, where they were met at Northolt airport by Peter Kemp, an anti-communist veteran of the Spanish Civil War, where he fought with the Carlists, a pro-Franco group also known as 'Requeté'. He had also fought in Albania during the war and been parachuted into Poland under the aegis of Harold Perkins. 'It was sheer coincidence that I offered my services to the "firm" just as this operation was getting started. I contacted Perks and he replied that he was looking for officers with Albanian experience. I had a TB complaint, but the "firm" doctor, Dr Lancaster, passed me as fit and my first job was to "nanny" these committee members when they came to London at the beginning of September 1949.'

Kemp's first problem was at Northolt airport, where he had to explain why Abas Kupi was carrying a revolver through customs. The weapon was temporarily confiscated. He then had to find enough food, in spite of an austere rationing system, to give a party for them at his flat near the BBC building in Portland Place. One afternoon his wife came home from Harrods store announcing triumphantly that she had obtained three pounds of ham pâté, only to be told that it was useless, since several of the visiting party were Moslems. 'However,' he says, 'Moslem or non-Moslem, they drank plenty of our alcohol.'

The aim of the party was to present the committee to some of London's leading writers and intellectuals, in the hope that they would publicise it. The whole atmosphere was spoilt, though, by Malcolm Muggeridge who declared in a loud voice that Albania was a ridiculous country anyway that ought to be partitioned as soon as possible between Greece and Yugoslavia. Nor did the evening provide much publicity for the Albanian cause apart from some brief reports in the London press. The evening's main disappointment, from the Albanian point of view, was the lack of any sign of official backing for their crusade. Kryeziu noticed gloomily that, apart from intelligence men, not one single Foreign Office person visited them or received them.

Julian Amery invited them for the day to his aunt Sadie Rodney's house in Penshurst, Kent, where lunch was enlivened by a political row between Frasheri and Kupi, the latter speaking only a tribal dialect that even Albanians could hardly comprehend. Amery remembers how they all went out into his garden for a walk after lunch. Kupi

David Smiley and his wife Moy with their two dogs, Dizzy and Minna, a photograph taken in Malta where the British set up their training camp for the Albanian operation. Smiley was one of four 'musketeers' (Julian Amery, Neil ('Billy') McLean and Alan Hare were the others) who enjoyed the Albanian exiles' absolute trust having fought with them in war and for them in peace. Smiley, who had stayed in the army after the war and was by 1949 second-in-command of his regiment, the Royal Horse Guards, ran the training camp with Moy acting as 'cipherene'.

Harold Perkins ('Perks' as he was known), the British SIS officer in charge. A master mariner who graduated from Prague university as an engineer, he ran a textile factory in Poland. During the war he was responsible for SOE operations in Poland, Czechoslovakia and Hungary.

Some of those involved in the British-sponsored landings. OPPOSITE PAGE TOP. Sam Barclay (left) and John Leatham, two ex-Naval officers, whose schooner, the *Stormie Seas,* transported the 'pixies', as the British called the Albanian guerillas, across the Adriatic. ABOVE. Four of the 'Pixies' on the first British landing: the Lepenica cousins, Hysen (second from left) and Sami (right), and the man between them, Zogoll Sheno, who were swiftly killed in an ambush; as the result of Philby's betrayal; the man on the left escaped. OPPOSITE PAGE RIGHT. Albanian trainees in Malta operating a pedal generator for their radio set. In the field it proved impractical, being too cumbersome (it weighed 20 kilograms) and vulnerable to the slightest knock.

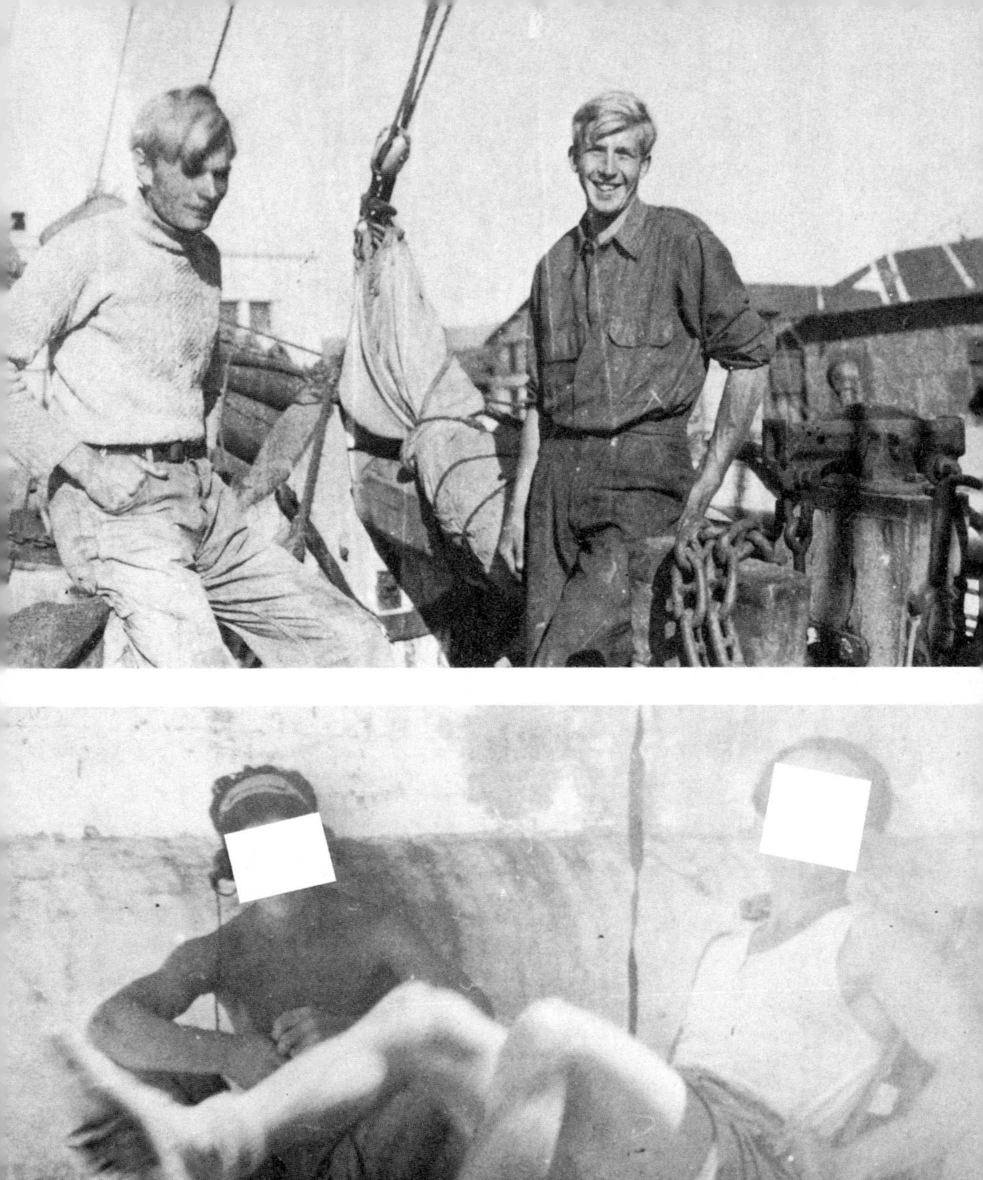

King Zog, Queen Geraldine and Prince Leka during their wartime exile in Britain. Zog, originally a government minister, rose to the Presidency and then became King in 1928. He was driven out of Albania by the Italians in 1939 and eventually died in Paris in 1961.

An official portrait of Enver Hoxha, who assumed power as the Communist dictator of Albania in 1944. A former teacher, he was born in 1908. An admirer of Stalin right up to the present day, he broke with the Soviet Union in the 1960s and maintains an isolationist foreign policy.

LEFT: Adem Gjura, leader of the first American-sponsored landings in Albania in November 1950. RIGHT: Hamit Matjani, famous Albanian resistance fighter and leader of the last American-sponsored operation, hanged in Tirana, April 1954.

Two Albanian volunteers, Hysen Sallku and Jusuf Dema, shown in the uniform of the American Labor Company ('Company 4000'), which was composed entirely of Albanian personnel. The double-headed eagle on the scarf badges is the Albanian national symbol.

US Colonel F.H. Dunn inspects 'Company 4000' at Hohenbrunn, near Munich in November 1950. BELOW. Albanian soldiers march near Munich where 'Company 4000' was charged with guarding an ammunition depot. The sign reads 'Welcome' in Albanian.

Harold ('Kim') Philby, whose appointment as Washington representative of the British SIS (under cover of First Secretary at the British embassy), ensured that the Anglo-American mission was betrayed. Recruited as a Soviet spy in the 1930s, he finally defected to the Soviet Union in 1963, where he now lives.

saw a snake. Using his peasant skill, he picked it up and carried it over to Frasheri, putting him in two minds over whether it was poisonous and whether he was going to let it strike. Frasheri ran and Kupi chased him round the garden with it.

Frasheri was welcomed at the BBC in Bush House by Hugh Carleton Greene, then in charge of broadcasting to eastern Europe, and given one of the daily fifteen-minute Albanian-language broadcasts to tell the people about his plans to throw the communists out. This too was reminiscent of the Second World War, when the BBC had been the main propaganda arm of anti-Nazi resistance. It was pointed out though that broadcasts to Albania were unlikely to produce any similar result. Few Albanians owned radios and the timing of the daily quarter-hour, 4.30 p.m. GMT, was inefficient, since the electricity supply was only switched on in Albanian towns ninety minutes later. In view of this Greene decided to ask the Foreign Office for a second fifteen-minute broadcast slot later in the evening, when the electricity worked. He pointed out that 'the present regime is facing a crisis' which provided 'a great opportunity for our broadcasts'.

Peers Carter replied on the Foreign Office's behalf agreeing with Greene's suggestion and proposing a new scheme, fifteen minutes of news followed by fifteen minutes of comment: 'Plain news may be regarded as a form of softening up, but the punch comes in as comment. And in their present situation the Albanians are probably worth punching.' The Foreign Office agreed that the extra broadcast would begin on October 2nd (within two days of the first landing of Smiley's men from Malta) at an additional cost of six hundred and fifteen pounds a year.

One of the Albanians working for the BBC, Anton Logoreci, went to see Frasheri at the Berkeley hotel in Piccadilly to express his reservations about Amery's idea of armed retaliation. The problem, in Logoreci's view, was that any armed attack would have to use Greece as a base.

And this in itself was enough to discredit the idea in most Albanians' eyes. It would be so easy to portray as traitors any group of Albanians entering the country or retreating into Greece, whoever their actual sponsors were. Anything they did would appear to serve the interest of the Greek territorial claim, in opposition to which all Albanians were united.

Logoreci met the five delegates several times and recalls, 'They were all in a thoughtful mood, not enthusiastic and exuberant, but puzzled and perhaps a little bewildered.' He was not told about any military plans and, though he assumed that an attack was being contemplated, he had no idea that it would begin in a few days. The doubts he expressed to Frasheri made their mark, he feels, but could not have any effect since the republican leader was already fully committed to the American and British scheme.

On September 11th Frasheri, Kupi and Kota flew to New York, Kryeziu and Pali had to stay behind. Kryeziu recalls that the first three had Albanian passports issued by the King's legation in Cairo, whereas he had no way of getting such a passport himself. (His and Zog's families were involved in a blood feud.) His travel document was no more than an identity card issued by a church organisation in Rome.

It was a problem that involved Robert Low in long hours of negotiation with the American immigration department, who reminded him that there were many millions of displaced persons wanting to enter the United States and they did not like attaching priceless visas to almost worthless documents. Low says, 'They kept asking us, "Why do you want us to give him a visa?" We said we couldn't tell them and they said, "Well, in that case we won't help you." And so it went on.'

Eventually visas for Kryeziu and Pali, who was in the same position, were issued and attached to their flimsy documents. They landed to refuel in Montreal and were asked by American immigration officers the reason for their visit. Pali replied in all honesty that they were visiting the United States 'for political reasons', whereupon the immigration men took fright and would not let them back on the aircraft. They spent two days in a Canadian hotel, appeared before a US immigration court and explained with the help of cuttings from London newspapers that their visit had America's blessing. It was several days before these protests, combined with Low's behind-the-scenes representations, eventually got them on a flight to New York's Idlewilde (now Kennedy) airport where they joined their three colleagues.

After the disappointment of their London visit, they began their American schedule with higher hopes. Frasheri told Low that, since his men were about to go to war against communism as America's allies, he wanted to meet and shake the hand of America's elected leader President Truman. Visibly shocked, Low told Frasheri that a visit to the secretary of state would be more useful and appropriate. (Acheson was, after all, responsible jointly with the National Security Council for OPC's secret operations.) Frasheri was adamant, however, and insisted that Low persevere with his request.

The Americans were less inhibited than the British about receiving the Albanian committee. It was done in New York and Washington not informally or by semi-amateurs but by the Committee for Free Europe (CFE), a substantial organisation founded three months earlier as a result of the early chills of Cold War. 'We look forward to the day when there will no longer be an Iron Curtain,' said CFE's chairman Joseph Grew, as he announced the committee's formation on June 1st, 1949. It was, according to the State Department, a private organisation with committee members well-known in American society, among them Allen Dulles and Dwight D. Eisenhower, and its clearly publicised aim was to collect émigrés from all eastern Europe into a political body and together cause the destruction of the Soviet orbit.

The State Department advised its main missions abroad that it had given 'unofficial approval'[33] to CFE objectives, that there would be cooperation and even coordination between them. However, in announcing that CFE would be financed by private contributions the State Department was being less than frank, since for more than twenty years CFE and its propaganda arm Radio Free Europe were funded mainly by American intelligence and operated under CIA supervision.

If therefore CFE looked after the Albanian committee, as they did when the delegates reached Washington, they were doing no more than they habitually did for Polish, Czechoslovak, Hungarian and other east European groups. It was a convenient way of maintaining intelligence control of the foreign delegates without arousing suspicion. Virginia Hall, an OSS heroine who had fought with the French resistance, hosted a reception for them on CFE's behalf. The Albanians were delighted with the occasion, which was attended by many well-known Americans and fellow victims of Stalinism, and they saw it as a sign that at last their efforts were being taken seriously. The next day (September 19th) the delegates were received by Llewelyn E. Thompson, deputy assistant secretary of state.

'It was a great honour and we were very pleased, especially since no one had invited us to the Foreign Office in London,' says Said Kryeziu. 'You must understand how we were. We were lost people, abandoned people, some of us only just out of refugee camps. It was a high point in our morale to be received by a representative of the American government. It indicated to us that something was really going to be done to free our country.'

The State Department meeting was not however what the delegates had expected. Thompson reacted negatively to Frasheri's proposal that they maintain regular contact. The American government was limited, he said, in what it could do for a committee like theirs and they would do better to keep in touch with a 'private organisation' like

CFE.[34] Anything indicating official American sponsorship of the committee would be exploited by other powers trying to embarrass both the United States and the committee itself.

There was further disappointment when Low contacted the White House with Frasheri's request and received the curt reply, 'Tell him to forget it.' Low could obtain nothing more, even after explaining his predicament, than the promise of a brief meeting with Acheson a month later. It was all very mystifying, Kryeziu recalls, to be thus consigned to the care of a supposedly private organisation after they had spent so many weeks being put together, looked after and paid for by official, though secret, American and British agents. They imagined that Thompson must be unaware of their talks in Rome and their clandestine military plans.

They were of course mistaken. 'Tommy' Thompson was a senior official and, however much he pretended not to be, well informed about every secret aspect. But when he met the Albanians he was reticent, or even evasive, since his government was resolved to distance itself publicly from every aspect of the operation, the political as well as the military. It suited the State Department that there was a so-called private organisation ready to take care of the Albanian guests and appear to be their sponsors. Then, if their adventure failed or caused America embarrassment, the government could land CFE with the responsibility and plausibly deny any knowledge of nefarious practice. The British had given the Albanians a poor welcome in London only because they had no such camouflaging device at their disposal.

Wisner, Lindsay, McCargar and other OPC men who had organised the visit and were paying for it kept well away from the delegates during their short Washington stay. They recall nevertheless the excitement of those days. The intelligence world had been talking for more than a year about striking back at the Soviet empire. At last they had received the political go-ahead and the men who were to be their agents in the matter were in Washington, living proof that something was actually going to happen. The first anti-Soviet military operation of the Cold War was about to take place. Others, it was assumed, would begin shortly. And there were many dedicated or ambitious Americans who wanted to take part and who shared the Albanian delegates' exhilaration.

Then tragedy struck. The delegates returned to New York. Kupi, Kryeziu and Pali flew back to Rome to resume their duties, Pali as editor for the committee's newspaper, the other two as junta members. Frasheri and Kota stayed in New York to set up the office. Low installed them at the Lexington hotel in Manhattan's Lexington Avenue. Several of Frasheri's American cousins came from outside New York to stay with him. Kryeziu remembers that the city was suffocatingly hot. He was worried about the effect of the heat and the strenuous activity of the past few days on a man of Frasheri's age and frailty.

In the early hours of October 3rd Low was telephoned by the New York police. They told him that there was a man dead in the Lexington hotel with a very strange unrecognisable passport and with his (Low's) name and telephone number in his jacket pocket. They wanted him to come to the hotel at once and when Low pointed out that it was the middle of the night they offered to send a 'paddy wagon' for him. Low said, 'OK, take it easy. I'll be there.' He reached the hotel to find the fulfilment of his worst fears. Midhat Frasheri, the linchpin of the fragile agreement he and his British colleagues had spent weeks negotiating in Rome, was lying on his bed, supposedly dead of a heart attack.

Low has vivid memories of the scene. There was his own despair at the idea of all those hours of wasted energy and diplomacy. There was the hotel manager begging everyone to talk quietly and get the body out of the hotel before his guests woke up. There were the police wanting to know who the dead man was and who was responsible for him.

And there were the Albanian relatives shouting at each other about Frasheri's missing purse of gold sovereigns.

The police wanted to know what language the men were speaking. Low did not want to say. They wanted to know who he was and why he was there. He said he was from the State Department and that Frasheri was an important foreign guest. He pacified the Albanian cousins by telling them to forget about the gold. 'It belonged to the American taxpayer anyway,' he says. 'I gave them enough money to have him decently buried. He'd come all that way to help us, poor old boy, and I didn't want him ending up in Potter's Field. Anyway, that was the end of our president of the next Albanian government.'

Doctors examined Frasheri's body, an inquest was held, a verdict of death by natural causes was pronounced. Still, even at the time Low thought it a bizarre coincidence for this key figure in the operation to die precisely when the first landings from Malta were in progress, a few hours from the moment when the first group were put ashore on the Karaburun peninsula by Leatham and Barclay.

In October 1949 it was hard to challenge the medical evidence presented at Frasheri's inquest. However, it was to emerge after the murder of various anti-Soviet personalities by Soviet agents who later defected to the West that the KGB had ways of simulating or bringing on a heart attack through the administration of a drug or gas. It was done, for instance, in Munich in 1959 by the Soviet agent Bohdan Stashynsky against the Ukrainian nationalist leaders Stepan Bandera and Lev Rebet, then in 1977 in London against the Bulgarian exile journalist Georgi Markov. Other murders, one presumes, were carried out more skilfully and remain undetected.

Low did not know either that there was a traitor at the operation's centre, a man who had been in London in September 1949 while Frasheri and his colleagues were there. The fact that Frasheri died while Philby was on board SS *Caronia* two days from Southampton en route for New

York (and therefore just a few days after his briefing on the Albanian plan in London) is yet another link in the exotic chain of coincidence. If he had known all this at the time, Low says, he would have ordered a much more thorough examination of Frasheri's body. However, as things are it must remain an open question whether or not this particular sudden death should be added to the long list of KGB murders.

6 Conflicting strategies

On September 23rd, 1949, President Truman and Prime Minister Attlee made an announcement that shocked the Western world. An atomic explosion had taken place inside the Soviet Union. Hardly anyone in the West had predicted that Russia would achieve this so soon. The United States and Britain played down the news, pointing out that the theoretical knowledge needed to produce the bomb was widespread, that all a nation required in addition was a scientific and industrial base together with the motivation to devote the appropriate money and effort to this one end. Still, both governments were deeply disturbed to know that Stalin had done this just at a time when East-West relations were deteriorating.

Albania was also a source of alarming news. Western newspapers claimed that Valona Bay, just across the strait from Otranto, was being developed into a submarine base, while its offshore two-square-mile island mountain was being turned into a Soviet fortress. Caves, galleries and other masterpieces of stonework were being hewn into the rock and German rockets, especially the V-2 that terrorised London in 1944, were being placed there to ensure Soviet control over the entrance to the Adriatic.

Once this was done, it was suggested, Stalin would use his new 'Gibraltar' to blockade Yugoslavia, eliminate Tito and reduce the country to a fiefdom. Russia would achieve her dream, a Mediterranean port, and would make the dream reality by setting up a client state in Macedonia, thus establishing an unbroken link from Russia through Rumania and Bulgaria, both of which she controlled already, to Albania's warm waters.

Stalin's behaviour, it seemed, was becoming more aggressive with every day that passed. On September 27th Laszlo Rajk, dismissed as Hungary's foreign minister earlier in the year, was hanged in Budapest as an American spy. In November a plenum of the Polish communist party was devoted to attacks on Władysław Gomułka and other 'nationalists' supposedly serving Western interests. Obviously they too would soon be arrested. On December 16th Traicho Kostov, former Bulgarian vice-premier, was also hanged for imaginary crimes.

Western intelligence leaders saw all the more reason therefore to retaliate and strike the Soviet empire at its weakest point. The removal of Albania from the Soviet orbit would be small compensation for the loss in 1948 of Czechoslovakia and China, but it would be a lesson to Stalin that the West too had the will to fight. It would also encourage anti-communists in the vassal states to follow the Albanian example by rebelling against Stalin's rule.

On September 14th 1949 the State Department submitted a twenty-one-page top secret report to the National Security Council on American policy towards what they now called the 'satellite states', inviting the American government in its first paragraph 'to reduce and eventually to cause the elimination of dominant Soviet influence in the satellite states of Albania, Bulgaria, Czechoslovakia, Hungary, Poland and Rumania'.[35]

Since the end of the war, the report observed, the United States's only achievements had been defensive. They had managed to check the westward advance of Soviet power and build up western Europe as a counterforce to communism. They should now think about reversing the trend and reducing Soviet influence in eastern Europe.

These were poor countries and none was very important, at least for the moment, but they were significant political and military adjuncts of Soviet influence, extending its power into the heart of Europe and forcing the reorientation of central European economies and cultures from the West to the East. According to the State Department, none of this enjoyed popular support in the countries concerned. On the contrary, it was deeply resented. The United States should react to this resentment and exploit it: 'The time is now ripe for us to place greater emphasis on the offensive . . .'

This was to be done by fostering communist heresy and nationalism among the satellites in the hope that they would follow the trail blazed by Yugoslavia in 1948. A Titoist government, even if communist, was better than a Stalinist government. Any movement from one to the other should be encouraged, not forgetting that the ultimate aim was to see even Titoist regimes replaced 'by non-totalitarian governments desirous of participating with good faith in the free world community'.

The US joint chiefs of staff replied to a second State Department paper (October 20th) specifically on Albania that the Soviet Union was still training Greek guerillas in Albania and building military works along the coast including a submarine base in Valona Bay that could be used for guerilla operations against Greek and Yugoslav islands. It was therefore important to deny the Soviet Union any military rights or bases in Albania and it must be a primary American objective to bring about 'the weakening and eventual elimination of the Soviet-dominated Hoxha regime'.[36]

Albania was again raised in Washington by Ernest Bevin at a meeting with Dean Acheson on September 14th. Bevin told Acheson, Gladwyn Jebb and Llewelyn Thompson that Britain's policy towards Hoxha was one of 'unrelenting hostility' and he was anxious to know 'whether we would basically agree that we try to bring down the Hoxha government when the occasion arises'. However, if Hoxha were removed, who would replace him? He was sceptical of the new committee and he told Acheson that what was needed was 'a person we could handle'. He asked, 'Are there any kings around that could be put in?'[37]

Acheson agreed with Bevin that a policy of eliminating Hoxha made more sense than any attempt to lure him down the Titoist path. He was not in favour, though, of 'precipitating' Hoxha's fall by taking more active steps to make trouble for him. He was concerned that, if Hoxha were to fall suddenly, the Greek army might seize the opportunity presented by victory over communist rebels and move into Albanian territory.

The Greek civil war had provided the West with a rare piece of good news. That summer government forces stormed communist strongholds in the Grammos and Vitsi mountains, driving the rebels across the Albanian border. It was, as things turned out, the decisive battle of the war. The communists never recovered from the defeat. This was not, though, appreciated at the time. For all that the West knew, Markos's men might be regrouping in Albania and preparing another assault.

There was therefore every reason for Greece to be interested in what the United States and Britain were doing so close to her border and the war zone. Apart from her territorial claims on Albania, she was keen to wipe out the rebels that Albania was sheltering.

On August 5th, 1949 Greek prime minister Alexander Diomedes told Moore Crosthwaite of the British embassy that 'he knew about the proposals for the establishment of an Albanian committee' and two days later London advised the Athens embassy of the committee's imminent formation in Paris, pointing out in all innocence that 'we have watched its development with benevolent approval'.[38]

The Foreign Office cabled the Rome embassy the same day: 'We are not playing up the formation of the committee in our publicity, as we do not want to lend any substance to the belief in Yugoslavia and elsewhere that the Western powers are behind it.'[39] The same disingenuous advice was given to American missions in Europe by Acheson. The committee arose, he said, 'on the initiative of anti-communist Albanian leaders'. The United States was naturally interested in the committee's objective to restore freedom and this objective ran parallel with that of other committees formed by Iron Curtain exiles. All these committees, he said, came under the umbrella of the Committee for Free Europe, which was 'a private organisation'.[40]

It would be counter-productive, the United States and Britain believed, to admit that it was they, not the Albanian exiles, who had initiated the committee and negotiated its composition. Also, if it became known that they were financing it, it would be easy for the communists to brand the exiles as paid foreign agents. It would also cause a diplomatic furore, not with the Soviet Union which was well aware of what was happening, but with neutral countries suspicious of such blatant Western interference in foreign lands.

They were anxious too about the effect of their activities on Albania's neighbours. The Greek army, flushed with victory, was anxious to punish Albania for her hostile behaviour during the civil war. And a leading article in *The Times* (London) on September 1st echoed growing British sympathy with the idea of letting Greece settle with Albania once and for all: 'Few people have been so strongly provoked as the Greeks have been by the Albanians. The UN observers testify that Greek soldiers, in advancing along the border, were punctilious in avoiding frontier violations at great cost to themselves. In many cases they were fired on from across the Albanian frontier, often by Albanian troops.'

During the Greek army's recent offensive, the article claimed, rebels in the Vitsi range near the meeting point of the three frontiers had retreated into Albania, made their way southwards, and crossed again into Greece to reinforce their comrades in the Grammos range. On September 16th the United Nations special committee's supplementary report pointed out that Albania was now the only one of

Greece's neighbours playing any serious part in the attempt to change the Greek government by force. It was a situation that Greece could not be expected to tolerate.

Panayotis Pipenelis, secretary-general of the Greek foreign office, told Robert Minor, now US chargé d'affaires in Athens, 'that Greek public opinion was becoming highly influenced over the Albanian issue and there must be some assurance to the Greeks that Albania would not serve for a third time as a base for a guerilla invasion of the Grammos'. There might well therefore be 'minor incidents' across the Albanian frontier.[41]

This idea was supported by 'hawkish' Foreign Office men like Anthony Rumbold, who was part of the secret Albanian plan, but it was not what the State Department wanted. Acheson told Bevin on September 14th of his concern that the Greeks and Yugoslavs might touch off serious trouble.[42] If Hoxha was removed immediately they might fall upon a destabilised Albania and satisfy their traditional desires.

Signs of equivocation in America's resolve to eliminate Hoxha appear also in a CIA pamphlet on Albania issued on December 15th, 1949. Its impressive array of facts based on all information known to the State Department and armed services, as well as CIA, in the period up to November 23rd appear to vie with one another for supremacy in the making of policy, as a result of which the paper reaches no solid conclusion either on the basic situation in Albania or on what should be done about it.

Was Hoxha's regime stable or unstable? Was it going to collapse? If so, when? And was such a collapse desirable? At the end of 1949 the CIA was either unable or unwilling to say, even in a paper which had to be 'destroyed by burning in accordance with applicable security regulations'. It seems strange in the light of the decision taken earlier in 1949 to remove Hoxha's regime by secret means.

The Albanian people were 90 per cent opposed to the government, the paper suggested. The communist party claimed a membership of only 45,000 – 3.9 per cent of the population – and a mere 5,000 of these could be classed by them as reliable. Living standards were the lowest in Europe and had declined since the Stalin-Tito rift. Almost everything was rationed and coupons were given out freely only to privileged administrators. Farmers and craftsmen received rations in exchange for deliveries of produce or manufactured goods.

Albania was a disunited country. Its people were Orthodox, Catholic or Moslem and now the government was requiring them to reject religion altogether. Traditional feuds and jealousies remained, even in the party, where the effect of former interior minister Koci Xoxe's execution in June 1949 had been cataclysmic. The land's mountainous character complicated central control and facilitated clandestine activity. The Albanian armed forces were 'incapable of offensive action against any foe, or of defensive operations against any neighbour'. Albania was isolated from the rest of the Soviet bloc and Tito was grooming the Kossovo minority for use against her. All these factors, the CIA claimed, led to the regime's 'basic instability'.

None of this, however, meant that Hoxha's fall was imminent. The Soviet Union had assumed the role of protector and their representative in Tirana, minister Chuvakin, maintained 'technical advisers' in every cabinet minister's office. It was Stalin who insisted on the appointment of Mehmet Shehu, who attended the Voroshilov military academy in Moscow during 1945–6, as interior minister in Xoxe's place. The internal security forces consisted of 15,000 carefully selected men and every chief of police had a Soviet adviser. There were an estimated 1,000 Soviet officers overseeing the Albanian administration.

The CIA believed that during 1949 Soviet ships had brought 1.5 million dollars worth of goods to Albania every month. Also since Soviet aircraft could no longer overfly Yugoslavia, Russia had established a weekly air service with Budapest for the use of their men. Heavier cargoes came by ship from Black Sea ports. Albania was important to Stalin's prestige, giving him a window into the Mediterranean and great strategic potential. He was capable of using it to put pressure on Yugoslavia or even Italy, as he had on Greece up to mid-1949. He was not going to let go of Albania easily.

The report's section on Albanian resistance makes gloomy reading and contrasts strangely with OPC's optimistic belief, as recalled by McCargar, that 'we had only to shake the trees and the ripe plums would fall'. Internal resistance was as yet unorganised and ineffective, it said, and the Committee for Free Albania (which was American intelligence's creation) seemed unrepresentative of the Albanian people. There was therefore no prospect of the regime being overthrown in the next few months or in the near future, certainly not until the committee succeeded in reconciling its widely divergent interests.

In spite of its high security classification, the report does not mention that a secret operation was under way to bring Hoxha down. It seems, in fact, to have been compiled by more theoretical members of the American secret service than the men of action in OPC, men with a far more hesitant approach to the operation that the government had authorised. The report bore little relation to the plans explained so enthusiastically by their agents to the exile leaders during the second half of 1949. And, now that the episode has passed, it confirms the exiles' feeling today that, rather than being recruited as genuine allies, they were used as guinea-pigs in some great experiment.

They were told in 1949 that American and British commitment to Hoxha's overthrow was whole-hearted, even if secret. But this was not the full story. In fact, the anti-Hoxha conspiracy was only a small element in the Western allies' Balkan policy. And, since Albania was the smallest Balkan country, it was liable at any time to be sacrificed in favour of more important American interests in Albania's larger neighbours. Western intelligence wanted the conspiracy to succeed, but they were not ready to pay a high price for any such success. They would not, as Acheson made clear to Bevin, turn a blind eye to Greek attacks on rebel camps across the Albanian border. Such attacks would hasten Hoxha's downfall, but they might also provoke Stalin to reactivate the Greek civil war. They were therefore too dangerous to contemplate.

Yugoslavia was a no less important part of the problem. The communist world had branded Tito a heretic. Stalin boasted that he would lift his little finger and Tito would disappear. Tito was therefore forced to look to the United States for help. Frank Lindsay says, 'It was only in the second half of 1949 that people started to take the Tito-Stalin break seriously. We then started to rearm him covertly. It was a good example of covert action supporting an overt policy. Tito told us that he wanted weapons badly, but not overtly, because this would give the Soviet Union a pretext for attacking him. We sent him five shiploads of weapons.'

Since Tito was largely dependent on American military aid, he could surely be persuaded to cooperate in the anti-Hoxha plan. The Albanian exiles very much hoped that he would do so. There were 500,000 Albanians living in Yugoslavia's Kossovo district, some say many more, ideal raw material for building an alternative to Hoxha's government. Both Yugoslavia and Greece desired the Albanian leader's collapse. It surely made sense for them to work with the West in achieving it.

Ihsan Toptani says, 'If Tito had cooperated, we could have had bases all along Albania's northern frontier. Albanians from Yugoslavia would have volunteered. Groups could have infiltrated and withdrawn on a large scale, collecting Albanians inside the country and creating a snowball effect. It would have given the people who wanted to fight against Hoxha somewhere to go and eventually broken the Hoxha government's morale.'

Tito would be especially interested, it was thought, in snuffing out this patch of Stalinism on his southern border.

It would make Yugoslavia more secure. As it was, Hoxha was playing his full part in the chorus of threatening abuse, orchestrated by Moscow, labelling Tito a successor of Hitler and lackey of American imperialism. If Stalin were to decide to overthrow Tito by force, Hoxha would undoubtedly assist him.

However, this was not the decision that Tito reached. On September 22nd he told American ambassador Cavendish W. Cannon, 'It is their business how Albanians manage their affairs as long as other people keep out of it.'[43] On November 2nd he told British ambassador Charles Peake, 'The Albanians were all out to provoke frontier incidents and to do everything in their power to provoke Yugoslavia into some action that could be represented as aggression.' He was afraid, he told the British ambassador, that Moscow might engineer a coup in Tirana and accuse Tito of being behind it. Stalin would then have the excuse he was looking for and would attack him. On December 21st Yugoslav foreign minister Edward Kardelj told Peake, 'It would be fatal for Yugoslavia to intervene [in Albania], since this might give the Russians the pretext they were seeking.'[44]

Tito was not being entirely frank with the ambassadors. He *was* interfering in Albania, using as his agents Albanians from Kossovo, among them Said Kryeziu's brother Gani. They set up their own committee in Prizren, near the northern Albanian border, and agitated for a return to Albanian-Yugoslav friendship. They also sent agents across the border. They did not, however, in any way coordinate their activities with the Rome committee.

Hoxha, on the other hand, saw little reason to distinguish between the enemies that surrounded him. He simply denounced them all as traitors and foreign agents. The appetite of the curs was whetted, he said in Shkodër on September 15th; the imperialists were busy putting their kennels in working order, recruiting for the purpose a well-known group of Albanian war criminals, torturers, fascists and murderers. He warned his people that Albania would shortly be attacked by the combined forces of the United States, Britain, Italy, Yugoslavia, Greece and the Vatican.

On November 21st he accused Yugoslavia of carrying out 119 armed incursions into northern and eastern Albanian territory. It was all part of a system of armed provocations, he said, coordinated with the Greek 'monarcho-fascists' in the south. He reminded listeners of the close wartime links between the Kryeziu brothers and British agents. He said that the local party secretary in Mirdita, Bardhok Biba, had been murdered by 'war criminals' parachuted into the country by the Yugoslav interior minister Alexander Ranković's secret police, the HUDBA, and that Tito was acting 'with the moral, political and material support of Anglo-US imperialism'.

The British embassy in Belgrade reported 'very considerable unrest'[45] in northern Albania, noting that it was no longer government policy to conceal this fact from the people. On October 24th Mehmet Shehu, now minister of the interior, spoke about the intensification of class struggle and of 'internal reactionaries' planning to overthrow the people's power. There had been 'acts of sabotage on a large scale', especially in the coal mines and railways, and several party officials had been murdered.[46]

Italian minister Formentini, one of the few Western diplomats remaining, was confined to one-sixth of the country and treated like a leper by local people. He reported much misery and constant rumours of political plots. On January 30th the *Daily Telegraph* (London) reported mutiny in the Albanian army and a purge involving 200 officers. A Greek newspaper wrote of Albanians wearing shoes made of cardboard and wire instead of leather and thread. A levy on farmers had just been imposed: 100 lek for a hen, 300 lek for a goat, 500 lek for a fruit tree, 1,000 lek for a horse or cow.[47]

Sali Toptani, who escaped from Albania in 1951, recalls what it was like to be a 'reactionary element' under Hoxha's rule in those days: 'I had problems all the time, just because

I was a member of the Toptani family. I served in the army from 1948 to 1950 and was dishonourably discharged even though I never broke a single rule.' One morning a relative of his, Veli Bey Juba, was arrested for currency speculation. Toptani recalls going round to Juba's house that same afternoon to see if he could help, only to find that the man had already been tried, convicted and executed.

Bame Morava,[48] who lived near Korçë until March 1951, remembers his military service manning anti-aircraft guns in Tirana from 1947 to 1949: 'Things were bad after the war, but after the break with Tito they got much worse. We had no shoes, no proper clothes and very tough discipline. A man could be arrested and executed just for complaining about the food. This was to panic people, to crush the soldiers' resistance.'

In September 1949 he left the army and went home to his family farm which had meanwhile been taken over by the state: 'I went where I was sent, one week in the fields, then the cows, then the sheep, the next week making a road, the next cutting wood. It was not much different from the army.' It was the time of British-sponsored mini-invasions with aircraft flying over the Korçë area dropping anti-Hoxha leaflets: 'I was thrilled. My grandfather and several uncles had been executed by the communists. One of my brothers was in jail. We were working and getting nowhere. Those leaflets gave us hope.'

He remembers how tight was the control exercised by Hoxha's police over every aspect of daily life. If he wanted to send a letter, he had to go to the main post office, stand in line and hand it through a window in an open envelope. The man might then ask him why he wanted to send the letter. Then he gave the man fifteen leks to mail the letter. There were no mail boxes. If he wanted to travel to another city, he had to get a permit and have it stamped in the place being visited. A bus travelling from Korçë to Gjirokaster would be stopped three or four times on the way while permits were checked and police would come looking for anyone who did not spend the night in the place marked on the form.

'No country was ever controlled as much as we were,' he says. Their family was marked as unreliable. He and his brothers concluded that they were the next generation that was going to be arrested. It was only a matter of months before it was their turn. The anti-Hoxha leaflets falling from the skies were for him a first indication that his life held any sort of future. He made up his mind to leave Albania and join the guerilla fighters.

The United States was hardening its attitude towards the communist threat. On December 8th, 1949 the National Security Council reported to President Truman in tough, far-reaching terms: 'The United States should do what it can practicably, particularly through covert operations and propaganda, to keep alive the anti-communist sentiment and hope of those making up the non-communist majorities in the satellite countries. To do less would be to sacrifice the moral basis of the United States leadership of free people.'[49]

Two or three words have been 'whited out' from the National Archives version of the report's final section which outlines the methods to be used in fighting Stalin's policies. It reads: 'Economic operations under the control or influence of the United States, skilfully employed, might in time and in conjunction with other operations such as psychological . . . operations, be effective in helping to weaken the Soviet-satellite relationship.'

The removal of a few words from the publicly available version of the paper is designed presumably to conceal a reference to OPC-style subversion and guerilla warfare against communist regimes. The United States government still feels obliged to obey the terms of the June 1948 directive establishing OPC that makes plausible denial a condition of any covert operation. It is unwilling to admit that it sponsored any such military adventure overseas, even thirty-five years after the event, even when further denial is no longer plausible.

By the beginning of 1950, in spite of the State Department's natural reluctance to use undiplomatic means, in spite of CIA's suspicions about the wisdom of OPC's subversive undertakings, the Americans were ready to take a more active part in the Albanian conspiracy. A mood of anger was sweeping the country, a feeling of panic at the dramatic gains that the Soviet Union had apparently achieved without any visible American response. The West had lost Czechoslovakia and China, nearly lost West Berlin and Greece. The West had lost its monopoly in nuclear weaponry, partly as a result of treasonable acts by American and British citizens.

Scapegoats were needed to explain the fact that American power in the world was no longer unchallengeable. The movement known as 'McCarthyism' was part of this reaction. It expressed the widely held view that the United States had done little to exploit her four years of post-war military and economic pre-eminence, that by adopting a defensive and over-generous attitude towards the outside world she had wasted an opportunity to neutralise communist aggression once and for all. And why had this been allowed to happen? It had happened, many Americans felt, because there were men in government, especially in the State Department, whose determination to fight the communist threat was less than whole-hearted.

On February 21st, 1950, Joe McCarthy kept the United States Senate up late with a six-hour lecture about communists in the American government. Without naming names, he referred to eighty-one individual cases of alleged disloyalty, including 'one of our foreign ministers' and a staff member working for an assistant secretary of state. A week later Dean Acheson was under attack for his friendship with the disgraced official Alger Hiss, for saying that since Hiss was his friend he would not abandon him. On March 21st Senate minority leader Kenneth Wherry called Acheson 'a bad security risk'. A special Senate sub-committee began hearings on suspect State Department officials.

This unpleasant atmosphere undoubtedly strengthened American intelligence's resolve to proceed with the one operation in which their soldiers were to confront communism militarily. The Albanian plan was, it is true, armed conflict on a very small scale, but at least it could be brought forward as an argument against those in the know who complained about American passivity. The necessity of 'doing something' against Stalin consumed all other requirements. The British landings had not succeeded. Frasheri's death had caused further delay. Still, the Cold War had to be fought, for reasons of internal as well as external politics. The OPC men running the Albanian operation were ordered to get their men into the field as soon as they decently could.

7 The CIA prepares its men

In July 1949 OPC/CIA appointed their first operational officer to go to Europe and organise the Albanian guerilla force. He was Michael Burke, an OSS veteran who had served in Algiers in 1942, then in Sicily and southern Italy. In July 1944 he was parachuted into Haute Saône in France's Vosges district where he worked with the resistance before being overrun by American forces in October. He then worked in the OSS office at 70 Grosvenor Street, London, arranging to send allied agents into Germany to hasten Hitler's collapse.

Frank Lindsay, OPC's European director, chose Burke for the job on the basis of this impressive wartime experience and arranged for him to be sounded out by his deputy Jim McCargar at a meeting in Washington's Stadler Hilton hotel. At the time Burke was no longer in government service. He had worked for a spell with Warner Brothers in Hollywood and was living in New York as a freelance writer. He had no idea who McCargar was or what was to be the subject of the meeting, only that it was set up on Lindsay's suggestion and therefore something to be taken seriously.

McCargar began to talk in theoretical fashion. What country did Burke think could most easily be prised away from the Soviet bloc? Burke replied that Yugoslavia was the communist country that appeared in greatest difficulty. Tito was still thought of by many as the West's adversary, in spite of his quarrel with Stalin, which people suspected might be a charade designed to impress the United States and tempt it into supplying Tito with valuable items.

McCargar explained that it was not Yugoslavia but Albania that he had in mind. Burke protested that he knew nothing about Albania. McCargar replied that this did not matter. They were not looking for a political specialist. The British had plenty of political specialists. They were looking for an operational officer, someone to deal with boats, guns, aircraft, landing places and money.

McCargar continued to theorise. This was to be a clinical case, an experiment in Cold War activity. And the aim was to discover whether it was possible to remove, in modern terms to 'destabilise', a communist government by a combination of open political and secret paramilitary acts. It was something that had never been tried before in peacetime and the American government was not sure that it could work. But they considered it worth a try, they had no shortage of Albanian volunteers and they wanted Burke to start immediately.

He left for Rome in mid-August 1949. His job was not only to act as intermediary between CIA/OPC and the Albanian committee, but also to supervise the selection and training of men who were to enter Albania under arms. He took up the contacts that Robert Low had made before leaving for New York. He was ordered to keep well away from the American embassy. He was given telegram facilities and money, but very little else, nothing that could link him publicly with the American official world and cause it embarrassment if his activities ever became known. He was not even given a 'cover'. He created his own, appointing himself the Rome representative of 'Imperial Films', an organisation consisting only of headed writing paper and a box number in New York. It was a plausible device, because there was a rebirth of the Italian film industry and Rome was full of entrepreneurs looking for a breakthrough.

On October 11th he flew to London, as had Low four months earlier, to be briefed by the Broadway men and the 'old Albanian hands', after which he returned to Rome and carried on with his preparations, assisted by Peter

Kemp, who was there as SIS representative, and then by John Hibberdine, who came out when Kemp fell ill with tuberculosis. He wanted to visit Malta, but was advised not to do so for security reasons. He supervised the committee's early months. His remuneration, $15,000 a year, was nearly ten times what Barclay's or Leatham's had been.

The American operations were more ambitious than the British ones, but they were based on the same premise, that a small well-armed group could survive in Albania by moving from valley to valley, contacting friends, living off the country, building cells, distributing propaganda, radioing back information and preparing the local people for more substantial deliveries of men and supplies as soon as the path was clear.

The scheme's planners decided to exploit the United States's position as the occupying power in southern Germany. The American zone of Germany was governed by a high commissioner, John McCloy, who was based in Frankfurt and advised by (among others) his chief aide Alan Gerhart, his State Department representative Alan Lightner and his CIA 'special adviser' Lawrence de Neufville. It was de Neufville who thought up the idea of disguising the recruits for subversive operations in Albania by assigning them to a special 'labor battalion' under American army command.

There were substantial occupation forces in the American zone and attached to those forces there were units of displaced persons from all east European countries. These 'labor battalions' carried out public works in Germany's ruined towns. They repaired roads, cleared rubble and helped prepare for national reconstruction. They also carried out some of the American army's less attractive tasks, cleaning army premises and guarding supply depots.

It would therefore be quite reasonable to establish an Albanian labor battalion. It would arouse no comment whatever. The Western public might not know much about Albania, but they had heard the name, they knew it was in eastern Europe, that it had been taken over by the communists. This was why western Europe was full of its refugees, unfortunate penniless men who had lost their families and homes. It made sense to take them out of the camps and give them work.

And so was born the idea of 'Company 4000', a unit of 250 Albanian refugees under American command with a substructure of Albanian officers, sergeants and corporals. Its members were selected along political lines, like the committee itself: two-fifths royalist, two-fifths Balli Kombëtar and one-fifth independent. They would receive basic military training and serve guard duty near Munich, but their main function would be to provide recruits to be trained in guerilla warfare by American officers and then parachuted into Albania's northern or central provinces.

It was Burke's job to find the school. He took the Scandinavian Express train from Rome to the Swiss border at Chiasso, then into Germany, past Munich and Frankfurt to Heidelberg, where he contacted CIA representative Roland E. Dulin. He outlined his requirement – a large house with substantial grounds in secluded country. There must be good living conditions, the same as he had enjoyed during his own training at the Royal Air Force parachute school at Ringway in England. He wanted a place that could be effectively guarded and without distinguishing landmarks. The school's location was to be kept a tight secret, even from the Albanian trainees. He could not run the risk of one of the men being captured and, under torture, revealing its whereabouts to the Albanian and Soviet police.

Dulin duly found the house, later known as the 'schloss', a large walled villa perched high on a hill just outside Heidelberg overlooking the River Necker. The house and its spacious grounds were made ready for the students' arrival, American instructors in guerilla warfare were recruited and the scheme then cleared by de Neufville, acting as CIA/OPC's 'ambassador', with McCloy's staff. Gerhart, anxious to protect the High Commissioner from diplomatic embarrassment, made one stipulation. The trainees must be isolated from the rest of the world as soon as they entered the school. Also, once their training was complete and they left the school to go into the field, they were never to return to Germany. If they did, they might reveal what they had seen and done. All sorts of trouble would ensue.

The next task was to recruit the 250 men for the company and this was done mainly by the junta – Kupi, Ermenji and Kryeziu – meeting regularly in their secretary Gaqi Gogo's spacious flat in Piazza Santiago di Cile, Rome. Burke oversaw the selection, but took little part in it. It was agreed that the Albanians themselves would select their fighters, not the Americans, who had no means of evaluating the refugees or communicating with them.

Adem Gjura, a well-known fighter against fascist and communist alike, nominated twenty-five of his friends. The three junta members went to refugee camps looking for recruits. For security reasons they said only that the Americans were forming a labor battalion, but it soon became an open secret that something more ambitious was being planned. Halil Nerguti remembers how in May 1950, in a camp near Bari, he was told that young, fit men were needed to fight and free the country.

Nerguti explains, as do others who took part in the fight, that there was no question in his mind of refusing to volunteer. Firstly, his life in the camp was empty and fruitless. He was a man with little education, speaking no language but Albanian. He could see no future for himself. Life as a soldier, however dangerous, meant work, dignity and self-respect. Also he shared the deep anti-Hoxha commitment of the entire exile community and was ready to go to any lengths.

'We knew that they would retaliate against our families,' he says. 'In fact they did against my family. They shot my brother Hysen and my father died in one of their camps. But our eyes were open about this and we had to do what we did. It was the right moment. There were internal quarrels in Albania at that time, the Yugoslavs were out and the Russians were not fully in control. So it was realistic and we had high hopes. Unfortunately, we were betrayed.'

The junta appointed Çaush Ali Basho, a Ballist, as senior Albanian officer and Xhemal Laci, a monarchist, as his deputy. By June 1950 the recruits were assembled and Laci, a graduate of an Italian military academy and one of the few Albanians with formal military training, was on his way to Naples to meet the first batch of recruits. On June 5th at 11.30 a.m. forty-nine of them left by train for Germany. They reached the Brenner Pass the next day at noon, waited an hour at the Austrian border, then continued towards Munich, arriving at seven thirty-five that evening. They were taken in five trucks belonging to the International Refugee Organisation to a camp in the city where they spent the night. The next morning American military trucks took them to Karlsfeld barracks, fifteen miles from Munich.

The men were assigned to two barrack buildings. They were given an iron bed, blankets, a mattress and cutlery. On June 8th they received their labor battalion uniforms, blue with red shoulder flashes and a red scarf carrying the black Albanian eagle. They were introduced to their American commanding officer, Captain Thomas Mangelly, who told them that his father was an Albanian from Korçë who had emigrated to the United States: 'He is an old man now, but he thinks of Albania constantly,' he told the assembled company. The monarchists were then taken to meet the Balli Kombëtar supporters. They were all thrilled to find that their American commanding officer was a fellow Albanian.

They were then asked to sign a contract of service and assigned to three platoons, the first consisting entirely of monarchists under Xhemal Laci's command, the second of thirty Ballists under Sami Butka's command. The third platoon commanded by Kol Hiles, was a mixture of twelve monarchists, five Ballists and thirteen Said Kryeziu followers, known as Agrarians. They were given a medical examination and Laci recalls, 'We discovered that Vlash Kotori had TB, Hajrulla Ramadani had syphilis and Rapush Zotbelli had problems with his feet.' He was upset at the idea that men with such serious medical problems had been selected in the first place.

He wrote in his report,[50] 'I pointed out that it would have been better to recruit younger people, since age and good health are vital to our work.' These mistakes happened because of the American decision not to get involved in recruitment, since they had no means of judging one man from another, but to leave it to the junta to come up with the right men. As a result, pre-recruitment medical examinations were rudimentary. Most of the best Albanian soldiers, three with officer training, were tarnished with the Italian brush, so they were banned for political reasons. Laci was unusual, an Italian-trained officer with a clean record throughout the Mussolini occupation. The rest were tough, but not officer material, and many were illiterate.

On June 13th they began their training at Dachau, nine miles from Karlsfeld, with a programme of drill, physical training, first aid, use of arms and military law. Their job was to guard a huge German arms dump, one of the largest not destroyed by Allied bombing. After six weeks they moved from the Karlsfeld-Dachau area to Wetterhof, Hohenbrünn and Hohenkirche on the other side of Munich. Laci reported to Rome that his monarchist platoon had won two merits for cleanliness. He was determined, for reasons of émigré politics as well as military pride, to make his platoon the best in the company. Laci recalls an occasion when an American soldier was sent to test the effectiveness of the Albanian guard. He was caught by the guard while trying to penetrate the fence. However, they could not understand his words of explanation and their arrest was so enthusiastic that, when the Americans at last found him and rescued him, he was very nearly dead.

Reveille was at 6 a.m., after which they worked from

8 a.m. to noon and from 1 p.m. to 6 p.m. Their military training was basic. Albanians generally understand guns and it did not take them long to master the American automatic weapons, rifles and grenades. After that, they now recall, their work became boring. Ramazan Cenaj says, 'I joined the company not to guard ammunition, but to fight the communist regime. We wanted to be selected for missions.'

They received regular pay, though they complained that it was not what they had been promised on recruitment in Italy, most of which they spent on their free evenings in town, or at the company PX (canteen). There was music and dancing every Saturday night. They paid levies to their political parties and some sent money to their families in Italy, although most of them had no families in western Europe, only wives and children left behind in Albania. If they broke the rules, their pay was stopped. Laci's records for 1950–1 show fines of one day's pay for lateness on parade, three days' pay for sitting down while on guard, ten days' pay for fighting while playing cards or for bringing a woman into the barracks.

Private letters were sent by military channels to Rome to be censored by Albanian committee employees before forwarding. It was from these that the junta first learnt of problems in Company 4000. 'Captain Mangelly has been instructed to improve matters,' Gaqi Gogo wrote to Laci. There were problems over pay and a growing feeling that the Americans were directing the operation without informing the Rome committee. The junta was nevertheless determined to show the Americans the best aspects of Albanian behaviour. Gogo wrote, 'We have learnt that men have been going with females and have been drinking. Can you confirm this? Give fatherly advice to the men.'

Exile politics soon began to disturb the atmosphere seriously. Adem Gjura, appointed an officer and Laci's platoon second-in-command, accused Laci of falling under the influence of Major Basho and the Balli Kombëtar, whereas Laci made the same complaint against the

Americans and Captain Mangelly. Monarchist supporters even today complain about Mangelly's anti-Zog prejudices, blaming the republicanism either of the United States or of the Korçë region.

'He interfered with my training and my nominations for corporal and sergeant,' says Laci. 'This was a violation of the agreement between the committee and the sponsors, which said there should be no political discrimination in the company. I showed Mangelly the agreement and complained to Abas Kupi in Rome. Normally I would not have done such a thing, but he was talking to the soldiers, making politics with them, supporting Balli Kombëtar, treating the monarchists as second-class soldiers.'

As they waited in Munich for the missions to start, their friends training under British auspices were already on their way to the second round of the mini-invasion. In October 1949 the survivors of the first two landings retreated into Greece and surrendered to border guards. Philby writes, 'A few members of the party did succeed in straggling through to Greece, where they were extricated, with immense difficulty, from the clutches of the Greek security authorities who would have shot them for tuppence. The information they brought was almost wholly negative. It was clear, at least, that they had nowhere found arms open to welcome them.'[51]

Philby could well have added that he was himself one of the main reasons why the two incursions did not succeed. Still, the truth was not so discouraging to the British side as he makes out, even though Smiley admits, 'We had a hell of a job getting them out of Greek jails. The Greeks tend to hate Albanians.' The survivors reported that movement inside Albania, although difficult, was possible and that the local people, although cautious, were friendly. They were first interrogated by Niko Ceci, an Albanian employed by Greek intelligence, and Bido Kuka refused to admit to him that he came from a British camp in Malta: 'They asked about our uniforms. I said that they had been parachuted to us. We had side arms, but there was nothing strange about that. We said we were ordinary Albanians fleeing the country.'

The survivors, all Balli Kombëtar, were then given the bad news about Frasheri's death. Kuka stuck to his story and claimed to be Enver Zeneli, the name written into his forged Albanian indentity card. But other survivors appeared from Albania and told the Greeks the truth, after which Ceci came to him in his cell in Yanina police station and said, 'You're not Enver Zeneli. You're Bido Kuka.' He replied, 'If I'd told you that I was Bido Kuka, you'd have looked at my documents and said that I was Enver Zeneli.'

Bardhyl Gerveshi says, 'They didn't interrogate us properly. They never asked anything about Albania, just stupid things like how many Albanians wanted to be united with Greece. I wasn't interested. An Albanian is an Albanian and that's that.' Their orders from the British were to ask for a particular Greek officer by name and, when the officer arrived, to identify themselves by using a particular coded phrase. This officer would know about General Papagos's agreement with Britain and have enough authority to get them transferred back to the British in Athens. Until then they were to tell the Greeks as little as possible.

Eventually the officer came to Yanina jail. The following day a British officer appeared from Athens and asked them for a prearranged password, to show that they were the right men. They replied in Albanian, as they had been told, 'The sun is risen.' He collected them into a British military aircraft and flew them back to Athens.

They remembered staying in 'a very nice house' in Kifissia, a fashionable Athens suburb. Then Rollo Young and Jani Dilo flew in to escort them back to Malta. Ron Little, Smiley's batman, came too. When he saw the Albanian survivors at the airport, he moved forward to greet them, but Young held him back, afraid that any contact between a British soldier and the mysterious foreigners might be spotted by Greek airport employees. Many Greeks from northern Greece speak Albanian and some of them might have been sympathetic to the communists.

During the 1949–50 winter the Malta team evaluated their achievement with the help of the fifteen survivors. Jani Dilo recalls saying to Papajani, 'There is something wrong. Is it with you or with us?' He became disillusioned and on December 31st he left Malta for Rome, then emigrated to the United States, but there was no general feeling that the whole operation should cease because of one modest result. In April Smiley left Malta for Athens and a month later his place was taken by Anthony Northrop, another SOE veteran who had been dropped into Albania twice. They began preparations to send a third team into Albania, this time overland.

In early July 1950 'Doc' Zaehner and Abdyl Sino flew six men to Athens: Muharem Hito, Nezir Tomorri, Xhemal Aslani, Preparim Ali, Zeni Mançe and Sefer Muço. Sino remembers that Greek suspicions were aroused during their three-day stay at the British 'safe house' in Kifissia and when they arrived in Yanina airfield, to his horror, there were Greek photographers taking pictures of them getting off the aircraft. He asked Zaehner, 'What is this? A wedding?' A Greek officer reassured him that all was well. In fact, all was not well. The reception committee consisted of Niko Ceci and other agitators for the unification of northern Epirus with Greece, a branch of Greek intelligence that resented British activity on Greek territory and British interference in a Greek dispute.

Sino says, 'It is very hard to deal with the Greeks in such matters. Every second Greek is a prime minister. General Papagos knew about us and was with us, but you can make an agreement with one Greek authority and find that there's another that doesn't know about it or doesn't agree with it.' The Greeks took Sino and Zaehner to the local hotel, then drove the Albanian soldiers to the aliens' office, the *alagopon*, and locked them in a room. Sino went to see them later that day and was shocked to find them thirsty and sweating in Greece's midsummer heat, being treated no better than prisoners.

Sino explained to the Greeks angrily that his men were at war with the Hoxha regime, not with Greece, but the police refused to release them and there seemed no one to whom he could appeal: 'Zaehner was there, speaking his marvellous ancient Greek that they could hardly understand and drinking a little too much, but he was only a professor. He had no authority and he couldn't do anything. And I couldn't help either. I was only an Albanian.'

Sino noticed that he was being followed. The next day he went into a coffee house opposite the hotel. Two Greek policemen were sitting nearby. He felt a man creeping up behind him. He turned round and the man threw a handful of pepper into his face. Hardly able to see, he staggered out of the coffee house and back into the hotel. The policemen made no move to help him. When he recovered, he found himself a centre of gossip and rumour, with people of Yanina asking each other who he was, who the English professor was and who were the little men locked in the aliens' office.

Obviously the mission could not continue. Their intentions were no longer secret and someone, either a pro-Hoxha Albanian or a Greek communist, was bound to have reported these strange goings-on to Hoxha's police. The British had bungled the affair by failing to achieve effective coordination with Greek colleagues. Sino says, 'There were too many cooks stirring the pot. The Americans were training men in Germany. This was coordinated with the British side. But then you had the Italians training men in Naples and Bari, the Yugoslavs training men and the Greeks training men. None of this was coordinated. As far as I could see the only question was, who is going to get to Albania first?'

Zaehner and Sino collected their flock, took them to the

airfield and flew them back to Athens, where they spent the next two months vegetating in Kifissia while Smiley tried to sort out the mess. They could not be allowed out of the safe house, since officially they had not even entered Greece and they had no documents. Ron Little was told to grow his hair long and never to wear uniform, to look as little like a soldier as possible, and Smiley himself took pains to attend Athens social functions, so retaining his Malta 'cover' as a friendly cavalry officer with nothing much to do.

Pat Whinney, the Athens SIS station chief, was confused by the sudden increase in secret activity and, Smiley recalls, felt that the Albanian operators were treading on his toes. Dayrell Oakley-Hill was re-recruited into government service and sent out from London to organise the Athens angle, officially under Whinney's command, but in practice he too worked independently and reported to London directly. Whinney's chauffeur Reg Voyce did odd jobs for the Albanian team and helped keep them fed in comfortable seclusion while Smiley discussed with Greek colleagues how best to avoid a repetition of the Yanina debacle.

Zaehner spent the period staying with Frank Stallwood, Whinney's deputy, keeping them amused with his stories and eccentricities, like the time Stallwood's wife Cora found a drawer in his bedroom completely full of money, several hundred pounds. It was his pay, he said. He had been given it in cash by the station accounts' office, but he had no particular use for it. Then one evening in early September Zaehner called at the safe house with cheese, liver sausage and whisky. When supper was in full swing he asked them whether they were sorry not to have gone into Albania. They said they *were* sorry and Zaehner replied, 'That's good, because you'll be going back in again very soon.'

It was the flight to Yanina, British and Greek intelligence officers agreed, that had led to the collapse of the first attempt by attracting local attention. This time they drove up in a fleet of cars, one of them driven by Reg Voyce, escorted by Oakley-Hill, Abdyl Sino and friendly Greek officers. Oakley-Hill kept the men in order, calling them by their first names and shouting at them fiercely in the fluent Albanian he had learnt before the war as a senior officer in King Zog's gendarmerie.

They covered the last part of the journey on foot, with mules carrying the equipment up to three miles from the border when Oakley-Hill and Voyce had to stop and let the convoy proceed without them. (This was a rule laid down for all British intelligence men after the 'Venlo incident' of November 1939 when two agents in the Netherlands, S. Payne Best and R. H. Stevens, were snatched at the border with Nazi Germany, carried across and successfully squeezed for valuable information.) Sino remembers continuing with the men and two Greek officers right up to the border, a dried-up riverbed, and watching them walk slowly across through the darkness until they disappeared into a cornfield on the Albanian side.

British intelligence, once again through Barclay and Leatham of the *Stormie Seas*, was providing its agents with an item of extra support. They spent the 1949–50 winter between Greece and the Black Sea running mysterious cargoes to agents in Bulgaria, then returned to England on May 14th to attend the SIS training school near Gosport in Hampshire and learn about their new assignment. The camp was very hush hush, Barclay recalls, consisting of a high wire fence containing about twenty wooden huts full of weird scientists who never seemed to leave their desks.

The SIS scientists were working on an idea invented by the Japanese during the Second World War. They had made a type of balloon big enough and buoyant enough to carry a high-explosive bomb. Their ships would then carry the balloons and bombs most of the way across the northern Pacific Ocean and release them into the westerly prevailing winds. The idea was for the wind to carry them over the west coast of the United States, whereupon a fuse mechanism released the bombs. It was a hit-and-miss method and not very effective, as it turned out, although a few bombs did fall in the Seattle area, much to the alarm of American civilians who otherwise had no experience at all of having their cities bombed from the air.

'They had this extraordinary idea,' says Barclay. 'It was to shower Albania with leaflets. I like to think that it was thought up by Kim Philby. The boys in London presumably imagined a rain of pamphlets over Albanian towns with thousands of people picking them out of the air, reading them and then preparing themselves for the liberation that was to come.' It seemed to him, however, as someone familiar with the area, that the leaflets were most likely to land either in the sea or on Albania's bare mountains, since it would never be possible to time their release from the balloon to the exact moment when it hung over a town or village.

Leatham's and Barclay's first reaction when confronted with this plan, worked out by SIS scientists in every theoretical detail, was to burst into laughter, but Perkins assured them that it was a serious part of the West's anti-communist propaganda drive, something being practised along the length of the iron curtain under the auspices of the Committee for Free Europe. American intelligence, they were told, had sponsored a programme under which millions of leaflets, pamphlets and books were being sent by balloon into Poland, Czechoslovakia and Hungary. If they did not want the job, they need not accept it. If they took it, they were to treat it with proper care and respect.

The scientists conceived the ideas, but it was left to one of SIS's skilled mechanics, a former naval engine-room artificer, to put them into practice. Every piece of equipment had to be specially made. The hydrogen gas was made by dissolving carbide pellets in sea water kept in a tank described by Barclay as looking like a converted washing machine. It was then led out through a pipe into a jam jar containing two inches of water to act as a resistance and control the flow. A smaller pipe led from the jam jar to the nozzle of each balloon.

When the balloon was full of gas, a length of cigarette-lighter wick was attached to the nozzle and a one-pound packet of pamphlets attached to the wick, allowing an extra length to hang down below the pamphlets. It was this bottom end of wick that they had to light before letting go of the balloon. After about thirty minutes the spark reached the section of wick that held the packet under the balloon, the wick disintegrated, the packet burst, the balloon shot up into the sky and the pamphlets fluttered down to earth.

Leatham and Barclay felt that it would have made sense to seek Japanese advice on the project, since the idea was originally theirs, but they were told this could not be done for security reasons. The Japanese would have wondered why the British were asking such strange questions. So they finished their training course near Portsmouth and returned to Malta in time to set sail with the equipment and the first load of pamphlets on August 6th, 1950. They got within range of the Albanian coast, hove to and waited for the Broadway weather forecasters to advise them by radio of a favourable west wind.

They waited for two weeks. The fresh water tank ran dry and their only spare water came from a converted fuel tank, which began to smell horribly in the August heat. They explained to London that there was a risk someone might get ill through drinking bad water. They were reduced to drinking nothing but bottled beer, even cleaning their teeth with it. London ordered them to put into Bari. However, there was concern about the balloons and pamphlets, which made bulky cargo and could not easily be hidden or explained. London did not want the Italian police to find such mysterious stuff on board a British boat and the boys were therefore instructed to get rid of it. Before they touched land at Bari on August 24th all the balloons and pamphlets were dumped over the side.

They took on fresh water, sailed to Trieste, collected new supplies of balloons and pamphlets. On September 17th they sailed south and four days later, when twenty miles off Tirana, they were advised that the wind was right for ballooning. They moved in close to the three-mile limit, by which time their machinery was working and the 'washing machine' giving off gas. A few moments later their packets of pamphlets were floating away slowly on lengths of smouldering wick towards the Albanian shore. They then made for Malta as fast as they could, arriving on September 28th. Three weeks later they were in Piraeus.

British intelligence then paid Barclay and Leatham off. They gave them a terminal bonus of five hundred pounds each and they wrote off the work done at their expense to *Stormie Seas* in Malta, including installation of the engine. It was, Barclay and Leatham felt, a reasonable remuneration, bearing in mind the satisfaction the job had given them at a turning-point in their young lives. Dino Mavros, their boatman, was taken on to the CIA payroll by Bill Brummell and Horace Fuller, who were preparing the American end of the operation in Athens. Derby Allen, who had helped row Albanians ashore the previous autumn, was transferred to the crew of a new boat under charter to SIS, the *Henrietta*, captained by a former RAF pilot, James Blackburn.

A twinge of jealousy appeared only when Barclay and Leatham were told that CIA had spent eighty thousand pounds on new engines for the *Henrietta* which were flown to Greece from Germany. She was a fast-moving ship, a converted German E-boat, and Blackburn was encouraged to use her between assignments on 'smuggling' trips out of Tangier to protect his cover and explain his presence up and down the Mediterranean. Leatham says, 'Whereas SIS were cheese-paring, CIA splashed money around, which was dangerous, because it attracted attention to the recipient.' It was, however, necessity rather than design that dictated this British thrift. Britain's broken economy and outdated industry could only support an intelligence service if agents were prepared to do dangerous work for modest wages.

The leaflet raids on Albanian territory, some by balloon, others dropped from CIA aircraft, did little to help the guerilla fighters. Muço's group were hiding in the mountains above the River Osumi on the way to Korçë when they awoke one morning to find the whole valley white with leaflets. Immediately the Communist Party ordered the police, soldiers, civilians and schoolchildren to go out and collect up the paper. They spent a day huddled in their cave, terrified that one of the paper-gatherers would find them.

They waited for a week to be joined by another group of three – Sami Bardha, Mustafa Doko and Petrit Butka. This too nearly led to disaster. Muço says,

> Bardha went to his home and his mother talked too much. She told people in the village that her son was staying with her. It didn't take long for the communists to find out and lay a trap for him. They persuaded a friend of the family to invite him one evening. He went there and they caught him. He invited us too, but they didn't catch us because I never went into an Albanian house. As soon as this happened, Butka and Doko retreated into Greece and we never made contact.

In early November, after nearly two months in Albania, Muço and his men crossed into Greece too. Oakley-Hill asked them why they had retreated so soon and Muço told him about the leaflets. At first Oakley-Hill refused to believe him. The drops had been coordinated with the Americans, he said, and had taken place in the Gjirokaster area, not the Korçë area. At this point Muço pulled from his pocket a handful of leaflets that Oakley-Hill took away with him, returning the next day full of apologies. The Americans agreed, he said, that they had made a mistake. Their pilot had followed the wrong river, the Osumi instead of the

Vjosa, and had released his packets over the wrong town. Muço pointed out that it was a mistake that could have cost him and his men their lives.

Towards the end of 1950 the survivors trickled back to Malta and, partly as a result of what they told their friends, morale at the fort declined alarmingly. It was clear that Hoxha's police had tightened their grip on the country and that it was now very hard for small groups to move about, harder than it had been in 1949. The fort buzzed with rumours. For instance, it was widely believed there that the Lepenica brothers, captured a year earlier, had been tied to the back of a jeep and dragged through the streets of Korçë until their bodies were reduced to bloody pulp.

An Albanian died of natural causes and Northrop was told that he could not receive a Christian burial in Malta. Any death required a certificate and it was politically 'not on' to issue such a certificate to an Albanian, since there were no Albanians on the island. Questions would be asked and there would be problems for the Maltese authorities. Northrop was told by army headquarters that he was 'on his own' and would have to dispose of the body as best he could. Eventually he enlisted Blackburn's services, took the dead man out in the *Henrietta* and buried him at sea.

An aura of doom began to surround the fort. Gone were the high hopes of the previous year. The Albanian trainees no longer seemed to believe that they would survive the battle and return to a liberated homeland. Northrop recalls that his men were highly motivated and willing to risk their lives, but they were not kamikaze pilots, they were not men with a death wish and they had no liking for what seemed likely to turn into suicide missions, especially when the objective for which they were going to die, Albania's freedom, seemed no longer possible:

> It was essential for the men to see the mission as potentially successful and therefore more important than their own lives. It got to a stage where they no longer felt

> this. As the months passed, they felt that they were more likely to die and that the mission was less likely to succeed. They wanted to fight, but then it struck them in the small hours of the night that in two or three weeks' time they were going to find themselves alone on a beach in hostile territory. At that point, yes, most of them were worried men.

One morning in late 1951 one of the trainees who had shown particular signs of depression disappeared from the fort. Search parties were sent out, confident in the knowledge that he could not have gone far on such a small island, and it was not long before Northrop found him sitting on a bench in Rabat's main square. Then, as he approached him, the man clapped his hand to his mouth. Suddenly Northrop remembered that the man, who was due to go on a mission, had a few days earlier been issued with the usual cyanide pill.

He grabbed the man by the throat and shouted to him to release the poisoned capsule. The man swallowed it nevertheless, but he was not able to chew it first. The trainees had been told that anyone who chewed the pill into small pieces before eating it would die in two or three minutes, whereas if the pill was swallowed whole it would take half-an-hour to dissolve in the stomach and take effect.

Northrop's wife Jean was summoned by telephone and within a few minutes she had brought the car to the square and taken the man to Imtarfa hospital nearby. The doctors went to work with a stomach pump and the man was saved, whereupon he was quickly removed from the island to avoid further despondency among the men.

Alastair Grant, the weapon-training expert, became obsessed with a local nurse. Smiley and Northrop remember him as a likeable man who lacked the ability to instil confidence in men about to face the ultimate test. He knew the job, but he was not the right man for it. Unrequited love, which he advertised at length to anyone at the fort who cared to listen, including Northrop's wife Jean, diminished his usefulness even more. Further problems arose as gossip spread about 'the funnies' up at the fort and 'the funny major' who never accepted invitations to cocktail parties.

Whereas Smiley had used personal charm and polo to cover up his real activities, Northrop found it easier to opt out of the social round. His cover as a major in the Royal Ulster Rifles was twice nearly blown, once at a reception when a woman remembered meeting him in London and taxed him with being a civil servant rather than an army officer, the second time when an enterprising corporal looked him up in the Army List, found his name missing and reported the fact to his Member of Parliament.

Then he too began to have doubts about the operation, its aims as well as its tactics. The Albanians started coming to him with worried questions. Did he really think that they had a chance of overthrowing the Hoxha regime? His reassurances rang more and more hollow as his own faith evaporated. The operation was being continued, he now believed, for political and bureaucratic reasons, with SIS parading it before other departments as their showpiece of anti-Soviet retaliation. It seemed to him that Broadway was experimenting with his young Albanian men, using them not as allies but as sacrificial lambs.

He began to see fundamental flaws in the operation's planning. Information gained from survivors of the two operations, October 1949 and September 1950, showed that Western intelligence underestimated Hoxha's control of the Albanian people and countryside. It did not mean that Hoxha was popular, but it meant that he had a tight grip and an effective police force, enough to make opposition seem futile. In such circumstances villagers would not welcome foreign agents arriving with illusory promises of liberation and free elections. The tradition of hospitality no longer applied. Greed and fear had taken its place and in each village there were men greedy or frightened enough to be ready to denounce their guests.

Anyone who sheltered in a house was taking a suicidal risk. These were bad conditions for guerilla warfare, far worse than under German occupation. As Mao Tse-tung put it, the 'water' of Albanian villages was not clear enough for the 'fish' of armed opposition to swim in and survive. The young men spent most of their time hiding or running, trying to stay a jump ahead of the police, with more than a passing thought for the day when they could retreat across the border. They did not carry out their programmes of recruitment, reconnaissance and sabotage. The programmes were impossible.

Smiley and Northrop taught them the demolition skills that they had used in Albania six years earlier. But would it really help to bring about Hoxha's downfall if they blew up a bridge or an electricity cable? Sabotage on so small a scale would hardly affect the economy, even the Albanian economy. It would be no more than a pinprick and the regime would brush it aside. It would not be seen as evidence of the West's determination to destroy communist power, since Britain would be certain to disavow any involvement, for fear of angering those socialists in Parliament who admired Stalin and disapproved of the North Atlantic alliance that Ernest Bevin had just negotiated.

Northrop believes now that the only tactic that could have affected the outcome was individual assassination. 'If some of the leaders could have been eliminated, even in a suicide mission, it would have been worth while,' he says. 'If Enver Hoxha or one of the men around him had been disposed of publicly, say by a man running up to him with a grenade and blowing them both to pieces, it would have had a great effect. And there were certainly men in my team with strong enough motivation to do it.' However, when he proposed this, Perkins told him that such an attack would be too 'noisy'. It was beyond the level of involvement authorised by Bevin's order. They must continue with small groups, symbolic acts of sabotage and propaganda – leaflets and radio. Northrop replied that operations based on such meagre acts would never succeed.

Other SIS executives, not Perkins or Jessica Aldridge, became impatient with this lack of result from the field and started blaming the failure on the 'pixies'. These little men, they said, were skulking in caves when they should be blowing up Hoxha's supply system. It made Northrop furious, especially since the critics were men who had never themselves operated in hostile territory.

They told him to step up the operation's pace, to get more and more men ashore and it struck him that some of them were reacting to pressure from above. They were urging him to hurry up and fulfil his timetable not for any good operational reason but because their prestige and their careers needed some visible sign of success in the field. The point came when he was no longer inclined to drop his trainees into Albania like corn into a mill without proper leadership or realistic planning, in order to save the faces of desk-bound SIS officers.

His dilemma did not reach crisis point. Other factors intervened. Britain's economic weakness, her inability to recover from the war's devastation on the basis of fifty-year-old machinery and trade unions, would not permit any launching of the grander style of operation that the Broadway hotheads craved. The simple fact was that, for financial reasons, the days of British influence in the Balkans were numbered. Americans were already helping the Malta programme with leaflet raids and finance for Blackburn's boat. They were about to send their own agents into the field.

In many parts of the world, including Greece, they were, with the British government's agreement, taking over Britain's international commitments. The Cold War was at its height, left-wingers were being hounded out of American public life and American groups were fighting in Korea. The conflict with Russia was becoming more and more America's conflict and in these circumstances it made no sense for Britain to keep the lion's share of responsibility for the little war that was going to destroy Hoxha's communist government.

Britain and the United States had begun the operation as equal partners, with British expertise balancing American finance, However, wartime experience and know-how were wasting assets. New techniques were coming into vogue and Britain could not keep up with her powerful ally in acquiring them. Britain had conceived the operation, brought the Americans in, handed over all available information, created the political base, recruited the first fighting men, trained them and put them into the field. The results had been mediocre, in some people's view minimal, so puny that the operation ought to be aborted.

This view did not prevail. Much had been invested in the operation. Careers were at stake. And Albania was, after all, the only place in Europe where Western agents were actually in armed conflict with a Stalinist regime. The operation would therefore continue on the understanding that the American side, represented by the Office for Policy Coordination, would take the lead. The British Secret Intelligence Service was to pass on the torch to the 'cousins' from across the ocean.

8 The first disastrous drops

In April 1950 James McCargar left OPC. The organisation which had begun in 1948 with ten employees was now 450 strong. Frank Wisner, its head, appointed Gratian Yatsevich as the new commander of the Albanian operation. Yatsevich's father had been from Poland, his mother Scottish. He spent his early years in England, before the family emigrated to the United States. He graduated from Harvard university and in 1935 went to Yugoslavia to manage a gold mine. In 1940, expecting the imminent arrival of the Nazi invaders, he blew up the mine and returned home to join the United States army.

During the war OSS wanted to use his knowledge of the Balkans and the Serbo-Croat language, but his commanding officer would not release him. Then a few days after the war ended he went to Moscow and served as an assistant military attaché under ambassadors Averell Harriman and Walter Bedell Smith. From 1946 he spent three years in Bulgaria, first with the Allied control commission and then as US military attaché. He had no knowledge of Albania, but many Albanians had worked in his Yugoslavian mine. As one of the few Americans with any specialist knowledge of the Balkan scene he was an obvious candidate for CIA/OPC recruitment and assignment to this particular project. He inherited McCargar's staff of four officers and ten secretaries and for more than a year worked closely with his co-commander Kim Philby coordinating American and British plans.

Yatsevich was a tougher kind of intelligence officer,

conservative in his politics and precise in his observance of rules. McCargar, he says, habitually arrived ten minutes late for OPC briefing meetings whereas he made a point of being five minutes early. However, he did no better than McCargar or anyone else in detecting that his British opposite number was a traitor: 'I found him immensely charming, very bright. He was, we were told, one of the new breed in the British service, more professional and therefore more trustworthy. This is why we talked to him so much.' Furthermore, he thought, Philby drank so much that he could not possibly be carrying on a double life. He remembers that after a particularly alcoholic dinner Philby came out to wave his guests goodbye, but had drunk so much that he fell backwards into the hedge. As Yatsevich and his wife walked away all they could see protruding from the dark background of the hedge was a pair of feet and one waving hand.

He visited the operation's European centres every four months: Rome, Athens, Munich and Heidelberg. He kept in close touch with Albanian committee members in New York. Frasheri's death had thrown them back into confusion and it was some months before a successor could be found. Eventually the choice was Hasan Dosti, another prominent Balli Kombëtar member who had briefly served in the wartime pro-Mussolini regime. For this reason McCargar objected to his appointment and so did many of the royalists who saw no reason why a republican should chair the committee. Xhemal Laci, for instance, believed that the new chairman should be Abas Kupi, the man who had fought the Italians in April 1939 and the communists in 1944–5. However, Wisner overruled them and by the early spring Yatsevich was busy encouraging the leaders of both main parties to provide recruits for guerilla training under Dosti's chairmanship and American sponsorship.

On June 25th, 1950, South Korea was invaded by communist forces from the north. Immediately South Korean premier Syngman Rhee appealed for help to General

Douglas MacArthur, then responsible for the government of Japan, and very soon American soldiers were fighting the Korean war. Only a few days earlier the Albanian labor battalion had been established near Munich. The North Korean invasion was seen by American intelligence as the latest of a long line of Stalin's outrages, a very good reason for speeding up their efforts to land Albanian agents on communist soil.

They had the agents, but how were they to deliver them? The British had landed their men from boats or put them across the Greek frontier. This had been possible, though, only because the men were Balli supporters whose families had lived in republican strongholds in the south. King Zog's support lay along the Mati estuary in central Albania east of Tirana, a long way from Greece and a long way from the sea. It would be a march of many weeks. OPC therefore decided to send them in by air, to parachute the small groups directly into the areas where they were best known.

But what aircraft were they to use? And who would fly them? The adventure was fraught with hazard. An aircraft was traceable through fuselage and engine numbers, which could be used to discover who was the owner and from whom it had been bought. Pilots were even more traceable. Stalin's police were expert at prising information out of prisoners. The moment an American intelligence aircraft flew over Albanian territory, both man and machine would be exposed to risk. And so would the American government's credibility as observers of international law in peacetime.

As far as the machines were concerned, the risk could be minimised by buying small aircraft for cash on the open market, usually Skymasters and de Havilland Beavers. When it came to the men, CIA and SIS had to consider firstly who were likely to be the best pilots on such dangerous missions and secondly what sort of pilot and crew would cause the least harm if they fell into communist hands.

The answer was close at hand. The Polish veterans of the Royal Air Force had contributed massively to the war effort, especially during the Battle of Britain when London was being bombed nightly and there were not enough British pilots to defend the city. When the war ended and Poland fell under communist control, most Polish RAF men rejected the idea of returning home while their country was under Soviet occupation. Famous for their bravery and hatred of communism, they stayed on in Britain, deeply disappointed men and as anxious as the Albanians to grasp any chance of fighting against Stalinist imperialism.

Harold Perkins, who had controlled secret operations in Poland during the war, was admirably placed to find the right recruits. The man for the job was Roman Rudkowski, an air force colonel who had parachuted into Poland in 1944 as an emissary from Britain to the Home Army, the main Polish resistance organisation. He and Peter Kemp, whom Perkins had also sent in, were there during the crucial period when the German army was on the retreat and the battle raged between communists and anti-communists for post-war control of the country.

Perkins and Rudkowski chose six of their most reliable men and offered them the chance to work for their American friends. They were to live in Athens and from time to time fly unmarked aircraft over Albanian territory, dropping men and materials to the resistance. The Americans explained to the Poles frankly that if they were shot down or forced to land in Albania they would deny any connection with them. The communist police would be left with nothing more than an unknown machine and a Polish crew whose links with the West could never be decisively proved, even if they were tortured and confessed all.

Alexander Kowalski,[52] one of the Polish pilots involved, says:

> We all fully accepted the fact that no one would protect us if we were caught. That was the deal. The Americans

> explained it all quite simply and they gave us cyanide pills just in case. All our clothes and equipment were made in eastern Europe. They even gave us Russian watches. Of course the communists would have known where we came from, but we were stateless and they could never have proved it. We would not have caused the West any great embarrassment.

Rudkowski was an archetypal Polish hero, short and broad-shouldered, remembered by Kowalski as 'a live-for-today fellow, a great drinker and womaniser' and by Peter Kemp as looking 'more like a character out of Murder Incorporated than the gallant and distinguished officer he was'.[53] A man of sixty, he was not expected to fly himself, but the six men who had flown with him and held him in particular esteem were chosen to go to the American air force base at Wiesbaden for a refresher course in the skills used a few years earlier to drop SOE and OSS agents into Nazi-occupied Europe.

Each flight was to have five Poles on board: a pilot, co-pilot and navigator, also a radio operator and dispatcher whose job it would be to hook up the static line of every Albanian parachutist and see him out of the aircraft door. After the course, in the autumn of 1950, the seven men were posted to Athens where they lived for two years in a CIA safe house under the watchful eyes of Horace 'Hod' Fuller, a local CIA employee, and Henry Maclean, the American deputy station chief famous for his consumption of ouzo.

The Albanian soldiers serving with Company 4000 at Wächterhof near Munich noticed by the late summer of 1950 that they were being given more interesting tasks than simply guarding ammunition dumps. They were taught to drive military vehicles and to repair their weapons, to cut barbed wire or electrified wire, to pole-vault across streams and climb ropes, to use passwords and operate radio equipment. American officers, anxious to find the best recruits for the actual missions, kept a close eye on them.

Then on October 11th American commanding officer Thomas Mangelly called in the two senior Albanian officers, Major Çaush Basho of Balli Kombëtar and Captain Xhemal Laci of the royalists, and read them a letter ordering the departure of the first group of men for the guerilla training school on the outskirts of Heidelberg. Laci reported back to junta commander Abas Kupi, 'We are told that they would be going to Albania to get in contact with the Albanian people.' He assumed, he wrote, that the order was issued by the junta and approved by the committee, but he was worried that he had not seen it himself, that it was communicated to him not directly but through the American sponsors.

The sixteen men selected came from all three political parties represented in the company. The royalists were Adem Gjura, Qazim Hoxha, Halil Nerguti, Sali Daliu, Llesh Nikolla, Rama Ali Beg, Iliaz Toptani, Agaj Daver, Xhetan Daci and Ramazan Cenaj. The Balli men were Mara Qemal, Sadik Bega, Harun Traga, Myftar Planeja. The Kryeziu supporters were Selim Daci and Rexh Berisha.

Laci's letter to Abas Kupi in Rome continued, 'In future, so as to avoid any misunderstanding or lack of responsibility on our part, I propose that no one should leave the company for any mission without your order or approval. This order should be given to us in writing, so as not to give the Americans a completely free hand to act arbitrarily.'

They were taken from Munich on a six-hour journey by covered truck at night-time. It was vital from the American point of view, in case any trainee was captured, for none of them to know where the school was situated. Eventually they drove up a winding hill and along a driveway to a fine large walled house set among trees, overlooking a river and a valley. It had been, they were told, a country retreat for Hitler and his close colleagues. Ramazan Cenaj says, 'It was a really beautiful place. I often see it in my dreams.'

This was the 'schloss' that Roland Dulin had earlier acquired at Burke's request. And it was here that the young Albanians were made ready for their very dangerous journey. Their American instructors were known to them only by pseudonyms. There was Major Emile, Albanian by origin, a man of strong personality and with huge biceps like a weightlifter's. There was Colonel Smith, and Major Wells, round-faced like a Slav, said to be a Pole, not in such good physical shape and with a glass eye that he took out from time to time to impress his students. There were three captains known as Raymond, Joseph and Giovanni.

Nerguti remembers night exercises in the hills surrounding the school, practising guerilla techniques and the use of two-way radios, also the three hours of daily physical training – drill, runs and route marches in full kit. They had political instruction on how to behave in Albania, how to approach people and talk to them. They were given pictures of all the main exile leaders, including King Zog and Hasan Dosti. They were told to find out first who was in favour of which party and then give them the right picture.

Iliaz Toptani describes lessons in map reading, use of compass, enciphering and deciphering of telegrams, unarmed combat, use of the grenade and the knife.[54] Cenaj recalls, 'One of the instructors gave me a knife and asked me to attack him, but I didn't even try. I knew he'd take it away from me. Albanians aren't used to knives. We use guns.'

The training, worked out on the basis of Second World War experience, was not as thorough as that given to British and American agents a few years earlier. The organisers were under pressure to get their young men ready for the field as quickly as possible. The Korean war was going badly and winter was closing in. If the men were not parachuted into the field soon the snow would start to fall and the missions would have to be postponed until spring came. It meant that there was time only for a training period of three weeks.

The men received no parachute instruction. There was not the time, there were no facilities near the school and the idea of teaching Albanians how to parachute in Germany presented serious security problems. One of the trainees recalls, 'We asked for parachute training, but the Americans refused. They said that one of us might break a leg. We replied that we would rather break a leg in Germany than while landing in Albania.'

They were taught how to land by parachute by being made to jump from a ten-foot-high platform on to a sawdust-covered floor. Later on a more sophisticated method was used, a winch that hauled a man in a seat up to a certain height on the end of a wire and then, at the press of a button, launched him into space. The Albanian trainees remember the technique vividly, especially the dreadful moment as they waited on the verge of being deprived of physical support, hoping that the split second before they hit the floor would be time enough to arrange their bodies in the correct position for a harmless and painless impact.

Gaqi Gogo visited the school with Kupi and Ermenji. Once again its whereabouts had to be concealed. They left Munich by car towards dusk and reached the school shortly before midnight. The next morning classes were interrupted while the trainees were presented to the three political leaders. They were given a chance to talk to the men. They encouraged them and discussed the formation of groups. Then after an evening meal, when it was dark, they were driven back to Munich. Gogo says, 'I am sure that the instruction was expert, that the officers were competent, but the period was too short and the trainees not up to the task either physically or mentally.'

Daci describes[55] how Giovanni, an Italian-American, gave them instruction in killing sentries soundlessly with a knife, in marksmanship and unarmed combat, including special tricks like how to disable a man by throwing dust in his face. The mission's aim was 'to establish links with men who were likely to help us and then to retreat leaving behind bases of men and equipment.' They were also told to collect information about the political balance in each assigned area, to discover how many supported communist power and how many were opposed, to estimate the level of industrial development and standard of living. They were to note the location of military units, arms dumps and particularly anti-aircraft defences as well as the state of local communications – width of roads and density of traffic.

All this they had to learn in less than a month. On November 6th, according to Iliaz Toptani, they were told that they would be taken to Rome to meet the committee. They were taken by car to Frankfurt aerodome early the following morning, while it was still dark. Dressed now in civilian clothes, the sixteen men were embarked in an unmarked four-engine aircraft painted completely black. They took off and flew south, but on passing over Rome and Naples they realised that their destination was elsewhere. The aircraft turned east and landed in Athens around midday. They disembarked, but as they were walking towards the airport building an American ran across to meet them in a state of considerable alarm. There had been a hitch, he explained. The Greek intelligence service representatives had not arrived. There was no one there to ease the Albanians' path through immigration control.

There was no way out of the problem. The Albanians did not carry passports or documents of any sort. It was only with the help of the Greek CIA that they could be allowed to enter the country. There was no time to send to Athens for help. Sixteen mysterious little men could not be kept hanging around the airport with no documents, even for half an hour. Questions would be asked, rumours would begin to spread and the secret would be out. The only solution was to put the men straight back onto the aircraft and fly them back to Germany.

Lawrence de Neufville, CIA/OPC representative in the High Commissioner's office, was advised as soon as the men reached Frankfurt, less than twenty-four hours after leaving it, and he was furious. The agreement between OPC and John McCloy specifically prohibited the return of any Albanian fighter to Germany once he had left the 'schloss'. It was, says de Neufville, the most embarrassing moment of his entire CIA career.

Two days later they set off again and this time their passage through Athens airport went smoothly. They were taken to a large villa where they found three of their party leaders: Gaqi Gogo for the monarchists, Zef Pali for Balli Kombëtar and Said Kryeziu. Michael Burke, 'Hod' Fuller and several other CIA/OPC men were there too and Robert Minor of the American embassy.

The Albanians stayed in a big house in an Athens suburb. Sali Daliu remembers a long corridor with rooms on either side of it where they all spent the nights, three to a room. During the day they never went out of the house. They stayed together and talked about what was going to happen. At this point several of them began to have doubts about the whole enterprise and the men due to drop into the Valona area, led by Sadik Bega, decided simply that they were not going to go. A day or two later the Kruja group under Qazim Hoxha made the same decision.

Ramazan Cenaj complained to Gogo about the hasty preparations for the mission and the lack of leadership. He asked, 'Why isn't there a member of the executive committee coming with us?' Gogo replied that this was only the start of the adventure, that the political leaders would follow after the ground was prepared. Burke too had his doubts, according to Gogo. He was worried about the possibility of failure, especially since so many of the volunteers had withdrawn.

American instructors, four of whom had come to Athens from the German training school, encouraged the others to persevere. They told them, according to Selim Daci, that the Albanian people were opposed to Hoxha's regime and would welcome them as liberators. They gave them forged

Albanian identity cards and documents identifying each man as a soldier of the Free Albanian Committee. These papers included an appeal to the local people to help the parachutists overthrow Hoxha's government.

Two of the four-man groups remained ready to make the jump and they were joined by Iliaz Toptani, a French Foreign Legion veteran, originally Qazim Hoxha's deputy in the Kruja group, who volunteered to go with Adem Gjura. And so on November 10th nine of the original sixteen were driven in a rickety truck hired by 'Hod' Fuller to an Athens military airfield. It was agreed that Adem Gjura, Sali Daliu, Selim Daci, Xhetan Daci and Iliaz Toptani would be dropped in the Martanesh area and that Myftar Planeja, Halil Nerguti, Ramazan Cenaj and Rexh Berisha would land further north near Kukës in the Lumë region. The Americans believed that anti-communist forces were still operating in these areas, that their agents would be able to make contact with these resistance forces, just as they themselves had during the Second World War.

The nine men got on board and, with the engines already running, Rudkowski asked permission to check that all was well with his five-man crew and say good-bye to them. He climbed on board and then, to the Americans' amazement and dismay, ordered the pilot to take off. It was a piece of typical Polish bravado. The night was cloudless and the moon faint, to prevent the plane's dark shape from being seen. They flew north across the Greek mainland. Around midnight, as they approached the Albanian border, the pilot reduced height. They were fifty feet from the ground when they crossed into communist airspace.

This was the technique used by all the American-sponsored pilots who flew regular 'overflight' missions to Soviet-bloc countries during the Cold War. It was never publicised by either side, but it went on for years. They dropped agents, supplies and propaganda. They flew from Wiesbaden over the Ukraine, from the Danish island of Bornholm over the Baltic republics, from Turkey over

Armenia and from Taiwan over China. They flew at chimney-top level to avoid detection by hostile radar.

Kowalski says, 'The Russians never protested about us because they did not want to advertise the fact of how easily we flew over Soviet territory. We went anywhere we wanted. We could have flown over Red Square if we'd felt like it. And you can do it in any old plane, so long as the pilot has quick enough reactions to stay no more than fifty feet from the ground. That's why the Russians are so frightened of Cruise missiles.'

Rudkowski and his men had no town lighting to guide them, since Albania had hardly any electricity. The navigator had worked out a route along rivers and valleys, using mountain peaks as markers. The aircraft was equipped with an electronic altimeter that gave out a 'bip-bip' sound to warn the pilot whenever the ground started to slope upwards. The co-pilot watched out for isolated trees, chimneys or churches.

The dangerous moment was when they reached the target area, the Martanesh plain, when the pilot had to climb to 500–800 feet to make the parachute drop. It was chosen as a place well known to Western intelligence. British agents had been dropped there in 1944, but the Polish navigator was still not able to pinpoint the spot where the drop ought to take place. They did not want to stay at that height for long because at that height hostile radar could detect them and once their position was known they would be attacked. After some minutes spent searching the ground without result they decided to return to base. The pilot turned his machine due west and within twenty minutes they were over the Adriatic. Two hours later they were back on the tarmac at the Athens airfield.

A week later (November 19th) they set out again, but they still could not find the Martanesh zone. By now Albanian and Polish nerves were at breaking point. They could not bear the thought of returning to base. So they held a hurried conference and a few seconds later decided to jump anyway. Daliu leapt from the plane. The pilot dived, the air pressure threw Daliu upwards and he saw the aircraft turning below him as his parachute opened. He landed with Gjura and the two Dacis in a wooded area near Bulqizë, twenty-five miles north-east of Tirana. There was no sign of Iliaz Toptani who was supposed to jump too or of their equipment which should have been thrown out after them.

The pilot flew on northwards with the four remaining Albanians for a further fifty miles at treetop level. They crossed the River Drin, climbed to the requisite height and tried to spot the small town of Degë in Albania's north-east corner. Again they could not find it. (The Poles complained on their return that there seemed to be three light bulbs that worked in the whole country.) Ought they to jump? Nerguti asked the navigator whether they might not be over Yugoslavia, in which case the jump would be a waste of time. Again the Albanian group conferred and again, on being assured that they were certainly in Albania and not far from the zone, they took the plunge, landing near Zarrisht twelve miles away.

Nerguti says:

> The pilot was meant to turn back and drop our equipment where he had dropped us, but he didn't do that, he just dropped it further on, the result being that it landed in another village entirely and we just had to abandon it. So we lost our radios, our food, our spare ammunition and all our survival kit. The Americans had packed everything into those heavy packs, even including toilet paper. We were left with what each man carried: a machine-gun, a pistol, a little ammunition and some simple medicines, diarrhoea pills and aspirins.

The Polish crew kicked out some packets of anti-Hoxha leaflets, the pilot turned west and soon they reached the safety of the Adriatic sea. Then a few minutes later, spotting the few lights that burned in the Albanian capital on his left side, he swung his machine landwards and flew it at rooftop height down the length of Tirana's main boulevard. They must certainly, one American says, have woken up the sleepiest concierge in the city. It was another piece of anti-Bolshevik Polish bravado calculated to thrill the air crew, even though it dismayed their American employers.

At last American intelligence had its men in the field, but they had landed with no one to receive them, not knowing where they were and with hardly any equipment. Gjura, Daliu and the two Dacis spent the night of November 19th/20th in a wood. They ate what little food they had and tried to work out what to do. In the early afternoon they heard voices and they realised there were men looking for them. They tried to hide, but they were spotted and a few minutes later they knew they were surrounded.

A man called on them to surrender. They exchanged a few quick words and agreed to make a dash for it. Anyone who survived would meet at a rendezvous point on a nearby hill. Gjura gave the word and they ran, the two Dacis to the left, Gjura and Daliu to the right. Shots rang out through the woods. Xhetan Daci fell dead and Selim Daci was captured. Gjura was hit in the leg, but he kept running.

Gjura and Daliu threw off their pursuers, gathered their breath and decided to make their way to Reç, Gjura's home village. But they did not know where they were and Gjura could only walk with difficulty. Daliu remembers how they came out of their hiding place every night and wandered this way and that through the darkness looking for landmarks. When they were hungry they called at an isolated house and asked for bread, leaving one gold napoleon at each place. They also asked for salt and sugar which Gjura used as medicines. He says, 'Normally we use tobacco on our wounds, but there wasn't any, so I made do with salt and sugar. The salt was to disinfect it, the sugar to anaesthetise it.'

They told the people in the houses that they were communist partisans, but the usual reply was, 'No, you're not partisans, you're the men the partisans are looking for.' Villagers would not turn them away, but they were far too afraid to help them. They just gave Gjura and Daliu what they asked for and begged them to leave. After a few such encounters they realised that it was only by a miracle that they were not killed or captured. The police had been thoroughly informed about their mission, including its timing and location, and had made every appropriate preparation.

Two days before they landed, they were told, several hundred security police had come to the Martanesh plain to wait for Gjura and his team to drop from the skies. They placed a man in every group of houses and were on constant alert during the night of November 19th/20th. Demir Manukaj, who used to live in the area, remembers asking the police why they were there. They told him that they had come to catch Adem Gjura. It was only because he missed the dropping zone that he had not fallen straight into their hands.

They made their way south to the outskirts of Elbasan where they found a friendly family who looked after them for two weeks. Gjura nursed his wound and they discussed how they should proceed. At first they talked about finding allies and continuing their mission, but by the end of the fortnight they concluded that it was hopeless and that their only hope of surviving now was to escape into Yugoslavia. By now it was snowing, but their padded uniforms protected them from the cold as they struggled eastwards.

One morning just before the end of December they stopped at a house in the border area. The owner offered to look after them for a week, but they mistrusted him and they left the house the same evening. They found a local man and in return for the huge sum of thirty gold napoleons he agreed to take them across the frontier. They crossed into Yugoslavia that same night after six weeks on the run.

The Albanian police, furious at having failed to catch Adem Gjura, the famous fighter, exacted a terrible revenge.

His cousin Rexhep Gjura and uncle Imer Leka were immediately shot. His immediate family as well as forty brothers, nephews and cousins were arrested and kept in such terrible conditions that within a short time most of them, including three of his children, were dead of malnutrition and disease. No wonder that Adem Gjura holds Kim Philby responsible for all these deaths: 'There could have been leaks about the operation from the Albanian side, it is true, but only Philby could have given them names, dates and places in such detail.'

He and Daliu were imprisoned in Yugoslavia for some months. As soon as he was released he sent coded messages to several committee members: 'Do not send any more packages to the original address, because they all get lost on the way.' He asked them to help him leave Yugoslavia, but nothing was done on his behalf and it was seventeen more years before he was able to emigrate from the closely supervised life that the Yugoslavs imposed on him. He now lives in New York.

He says, 'I do not agree with the way the operation was done, but if I got another chance I would do the same again, in spite of the members of my family that were killed, because I cannot tolerate Albania remaining under the communists.' In a recent letter he wrote, 'In spite of all the misery, the sacrifice was worth while for King and Country. I am sorry only that I failed in my mission. And for that reason my life is not worth anything any more.'

Meanwhile Iliaz Toptani had failed to make contact with the other members of the Gjura group. He took refuge in an Albanian house, but he was quickly denounced and captured. The Nerguti group were more fortunate because in their case the navigational error over where they were to be dropped was even greater than in the Gjura group's case. Zarrisht was no less than six hours march from Degë, the scheduled zone, the place that had been notified to the Albanians and where the police were waiting for them. Police in Zarrisht were alerted only when their equipment fell into the middle of the village. Within a few hours the village was surrounded and being searched, but by then Planeja, Nerguti, Berisha and Cenaj had taken refuge in the nearby forest.

The reason they were not caught, says Cenaj, is that they lay low in the forest for five days and nights, moving only enough to collect water from a stream, eating vitamin pills and the small amount of food that they carried on their person. Then, after checking with a local shepherd, to whom they gave five hundred leks, that the police patrols had gone elsewhere they set out eastwards to the border region of Has where they had friends and family.

They walked across the hills to Kishaj, a village near Krumë, called at an isolated house and were given food. Nerguti says, 'They were surprised and frightened, but they received us well and gave us enough food for a week.' They carried on marching, but it was December already and snowing. They sheltered in remote huts and stables, praying that the snow would not stop, in which case any footprint would reveal the presence of strangers. Their only consolation was that the snow also impeded the mobility of police and soldiers.

They hoped to reach Gjegjen, Nerguti's home village in the Lumë region. His brother and father were already under arrest. He hoped to find other members of his family and get them across the border. However, by mid-December the snow was so thick that they could no longer contemplate such a long march. They made for Mount Peshtrik which marks the border in Albania's north-east corner and crossed into Yugoslavia.

They made for the large town of Prizren ten miles inside Yugoslavia. Cenaj says, 'The local Albanians were thrilled to hear that we had been sent by the Americans. They saw us as very important people.' By February 1951 they had fourteen more volunteers ready to return to Albania and fight. Nerguti used his gold napoleons to buy arms for them. They re-entered the country in small groups towards the end of the month, successfully dodging Yugoslav and Albanian border patrols.

Cenaj recalls that his armed men were well received by the people who had been encouraged by broadcasts and leaflet raids to believe that at last something serious was happening. However, he says, disillusionment soon set in. Words were not being followed by deeds. The villagers expected equipment and men to be poured into the area, as had happened under German occupation, but weeks passed and nothing happened. Cenaj found himself being asked, 'Where are your American and English friends? Still up in the sky?'

During the spring of 1951 the men they had recruited were picked off one by one in various encounters with Albanian security forces. As usual the story of the Second World War was being repeated. People wanted tangible proof of American commitment to Hoxha's overthrow. Once they started getting parachute drops of men and weapons, they said, they would take up arms and join the fight. The drops never came and eventually disillusionment spread to the original four men. They decided that they would have to surrender. Greece was too far away. So they sent emissaries across the border to explain their position to the Yugoslav police. On May 9th they crossed over themselves and surrendered.

Three years later Cenaj was allowed to leave Yugoslavia, but Nerguti remained until 1963 when he and his family emigrated to France. Today in Paris he talks about the events of 1950–1 with deep sadness: 'Philby is responsible for great suffering. Because he betrayed my mission, there are a hundred families still in jail in Albania even now. He caused us to lose faith in our allies, to understand that we Albanians are a small country. We have few friends and the big powers don't care very much about us. We were used as an experiment. We were a small part of a big game, pawns that could be sacrificed.'

Nerguti's postcards to Gaqi Gogo from Yugoslavia were

the first news that reached OPC/CIA about their agents' fate. During the second half of November and early December 1950 Rudkowski's men flew over Martanesh and Has every four days trying to make contact with the groups through ground-to-air narrow-channel radio sets known colloquially as 'Joan-Eleanor', equipment used six years earlier in Mosquito bombers to communicate with Allied agents in Berlin and other German cities. It was rudimentary, which was just as well since the Albanians and Poles had no common language, just a few words of English between them. Of course, since no group was able to recover a radio from its parachuted equipment, no messages were sent or received. The Polish crews had to return to base time after time with nothing to report.

OPC/CIA decided nevertheless to quicken the pace of its operations. By the end of March 1951 there were thirteen new recruits at the training school and on June 8th a further twenty-seven were transferred there from the Wächterhof (Munich) labor battalion. Meanwhile British intelligence withdrew Peter Kemp and John Hibberdine from Rome, bringing Archie Lyall from Trieste to replace them. Burke also left the operation to replace Lawrence de Neufville as John McCloy's CIA special adviser in Frankfurt. The Albanian committee gave him a farewell dinner in Rome and all signed the menu. His place was taken by Joseph Leib, a former major in the American army and public relations specialist.

At this point, after the initial failures, relations between the Albanians and the Western allies began to deteriorate. It was based on an American feeling that, since they were paying for the operation, they were entitled to control its most important decisions, whereas the Albanians, the soldiers as well as the committee, wanted military decisions to be taken by their own junta. One of the trainees in Germany remembers saying to an American officer, 'Always remember that I'm not going to Albania to fight for you. For you I'll wash dishes in New York, if it turns out that I have to, but if I'm allowed to fight it will only be for Albania.'

Xhemal Laci says:

> The Americans who prepared our men for these missions knew nothing of Albania, the Albanian people or their mentality. We had served in the resistance. We knew the topography and the places that were best for preparatory raids. The Americans wasted all this knowledge. They did not know the Albanian proverb: 'If you have an itch, it is your own hand that knows best where to scratch.' At least the British enjoyed the experience of men who had fought in Albania in 1943–5. The Americans had no such experts, only some American officers of Albanian origin. And these were no substitute.

OPC/CIA began putting substantial sums of money into the operation. Much of it was channelled through Leib in Rome and distributed in a way that caused controversy and resentment. Leib lived in a large villa in the Frascati district with his wife Mildred, who was in poor health, a fact which did not prevent him spending frequent evenings in local casinos and nightclubs. He purchased a Papal title and sported it on his visiting cards, causing great merriment among the American community.

Gaqi Gogo does not agree with these criticisms: 'The Balli Kombëtar people criticised Leib for his high living and extravagance, but they were only too glad to get their share of any money that was going. Anyway, it would have made a bad impression on Albanians to have attempted things on the cheap. Money is very important in politics, especially Balkan politics.'

Abas Ermenji, on the other hand, believes strongly that Leib's style downgraded the whole enterprise and corrupted those who took part, many of them men from poor backgrounds who had spent the previous few years in refugee camps. His flamboyance attracted opportunists, men without patriotic commitment whose careless talk damaged the operation's security. Vasil Andoni says, 'There was far too much gossip in Rome bars about missions to Albania and who was going on them. Maybe they didn't realise it, but they were doing Philby's job for him.'

This was just as well, from Stalin's and Hoxha's point of view, because their master spy's usefulness was about to disappear. Since August 1950 there had been a guest at Philby's home, Guy Burgess, an outrageous figure on the London scene, a homosexual well known for his brilliant wit and scandalously drunken behaviour. It was indeed a strange decision on Philby's part to accommodate such a bizarre character who was also, he knew, like himself an agent of the Soviet Union. It was to lead very soon to his removal from the nerve-centre of American and British intelligence.

Burgess fitted in well with life at 5228 Nebraska Avenue, Washington. He was liked by Philby's wife Aileen and played trains with their children Josephine, John and Tommy. George Jellicoe recalls how he came to work late every morning, usually the worse for wear, and remembers particularly his 'ghastly fingernails'. His colourful behaviour was unsuited to any man attempting to lead a double life. In December he was ejected from the home of the American columnist Joseph Alsop for drunkenly gatecrashing a party.[56] In February 1951 the Virginia police stopped him for speeding three times in one day. The British embassy was told that his companion in the car was an American convicted of homosexual offences. It was around that time that Philby, suspecting that Burgess's days in Washington were numbered, told him that British security was closing its net around a third Soviet agent, Donald Maclean, then head of the Foreign Office's American Department.

In April Burgess was recalled to face a disciplinary board and on May 7th he arrived in Southampton on the *Queen Mary*. During the next few days, it is assumed, he tipped Maclean off about what Philby had told him, that Maclean was under suspicion, would shortly be arrested and would be best advised to make his way 'home' to Moscow. On May 25th, just before midnight, Maclean and Burgess took the night boat from Southampton and were soon in the land of their Russian employers. Philby was advised of this by telegram and was relieved to learn that Maclean had made good his escape. He concedes, however, that the news that Burgess had impulsively decided to flee with him caused him deep consternation.

A few days later he was recalled to London and after some weeks' delay subjected to an internal 'trial' before a barrister with top security clearance, Helenus Milmo, on the basis of evidence compiled by one of MI5's top men, Dick White. White and other British security officers were convinced of Philby's guilt. His association with the absurd Burgess was incomprehensible and his dramatic political shifts, ranging from extreme leftism at Cambridge university to pro-Franco journalism in the 1930s and membership of pro-Nazi organisations, simply did not hang together.

It was also becoming clear that various projects in which Philby was involved were ending in disaster. There was the unexplained disappearance of Konstantin Volkov, an important potential defector from the Soviet embassy in Turkey. And there was the conspicuous failure of the Albanian operation. CIA were by now deeply suspicious of him; its director Walter Bedell Smith demanded his removal, it is said, under threat of breaking off the American-British intelligence relationship.

Milmo's report concluded that Philby was probably guilty, but it provided no proof. It was, according to a senior M15 man involved in the investigation, the only possible verdict. Milmo had found Philby's explanations unsatisfactory, but he had not been able to break him. His stammer enabled him to hedge under cross-examination and think twice before answering every question. He knew how much MI5 knew, he was carefully trained and determined not to confess. It presented SIS boss Stewart Menzies with an agonising choice.

Menzies decided eventually to retire Philby from the secret service. Dick White, Walter Bedell Smith and many others were relieved, but the general view in SIS itself was that Philby had been sacrificed on the altar of American jealousy and McCarthyite bigotry. He spent the next two years at his home at Rickmansworth in Hertfordshire with his wife and four children – the youngest, Harry, had just been born – in an apparently miserable and humiliated state, complaining loudly of unfair treatment to any former colleague who agreed to listen.

That summer George Jellicoe, who was in London on his way from Washington to a new posting in Brussels, received a letter from his Foreign Office permanent secretary Derek Hoyer Millar advising him that Philby was suspected of disloyalty and ordering him to avoid Philby's company. 'I was outraged,' Jellicoe recalls. 'It struck me as McCarthyism at its worst. It was an order, so I obeyed it, but I didn't like what I was doing. I truly believed him innocent. I was completely deceived by him.'

However, while good friends were sympathetic in their innocence, SIS men in the know conceded that legitimate doubts over Philby's loyalty had been raised and it seems now hard to understand why, with CIA convinced of Philby's guilt and SIS suspicious of him, they nevertheless decided in mid-1951 to proceed with the 'secret' Albanian operation that for nearly two years, first with Jim McCargar and then with Gratian Yatsevich, Philby had jointly commanded.

The forty trainees at the Heidelberg school, twenty-seven of whom arrived on June 8th, went through another hurried course of instruction in preparation for the next series of parachute drops. On this occasion they received forty days training in guerilla warfare, twice as long as the previous group had, and on July 20th sixteen of them left for Athens as a prelude to being dropped into Albania in groups of four. One group, it was decided, would stay in Athens. Fidai Veli, Xhemal Riza, Kasem Shehu and Muhamet

Hoxha (no relation to the communist leaders) were to land near Gjirokaster; Murredin Lusha, Dilaver Kacuqi, Kalem Xhabexhiu and Ryfat Zyberi near Kavaja; Hamit Toshi, Ded Hila, Rusta Azis and Azis Azizaj near Shkodër.

Each man had his voice recorded on a gramophone. This was so that he could be identified when sending radio messages. They were shown detailed maps of their designated areas with points marked in red and black, the red marks indicating communist positions and the black marks indicating houses thought likely to welcome and assist the resistance. If an aircraft flew over them at night-time, they were told, they should light a fire in the vicinity and use their 'Joan-Eleanor' sets to communicate with it. There would be large numbers of local people ready to help them. They should recruit these people and build centres of resistance before retreating into Greece or Yugoslavia.[57]

The drop took place on July 23rd and was a total disaster. The four men from the Kavaja group were caught in a house. The police set fire to it and burned them to death. The Shkodër group was destroyed as soon as the four men landed. Kasem Shehu and Muhamet Hoxha were captured near Gjirokaster after the other two members of their group were killed. All this happened a month after Philby's recall and it is very hard to understand the decision to parachute the twelve men in while an inquiry into his loyalty was actually in progress.

On October 10th Shehu and Hoxha were brought to trial in Tirana's 'November 17th' cinema together with Selim Daci and Iliaẓ Toptani from the first American drop the previous November and ten other men charged with invading Albania under British, Greek, Italian or Yugoslav sponsorship. The twelve-day trial was interlaced with crude political propaganda interjected at strategic intervals by the prosecuting lawyer as he attempted to show, incorrectly, that the actions of the five invading nations were closely coordinated. It was characterised, as usual in Stalinist trials, by the abject zombie-like demeanour of defendants, tortured into semi-insanity, vilifying American or British imperialism and their own roles as imperialism's lackeys.

However, unlike the trials taking place in other east European countries at that time, with rehearsed or pre-recorded evidence being broadcast on national radio and from loudspeakers in public squares, the information that emerges from the 1951 Tirana trial was, in the author's view, essentially accurate, at least as regards the four American-sponsored defendants. The dates, names and other details appearing in the transcript put out by the Albanian government in 1952 do not generally conflict with the facts provided by Albanian and American participants thirty-three years after the trial.

The indictment by the public prosecutor, Sotir Qirjaqi, consisted of a long and extremely prejudicial statement: 'These servants of the proud sterling were unable to carry out their criminal and hostile plans to the people's detriment. They had not time to let off the explosive charges that they had been provided with by imperialist forces. Instead they found themselves surrounded by the security police, following which they were either annihilated or captured alive by the police or by local people.'[58] The lawyers for the defence were reduced to pleading in mitigation their clients' repentance and willingness to assist the police by revealing everything they knew about the operation. Other defence arguments were the cunning and skill of the accused men's American instructors and, in Iliaz Toptani's case, the burden that he carried as the product of an aristocratic background.

Vangjel Dhimo had allegedly been trained by the Greek 'Asfalia' (secret service) under British supervision before being put across the border to further the Greek claim to Albanian territory. Seid Bylykbashi had allegedly been trained by the Italian 'neo-fascists', also under British direction. Both were sentenced to death. Of the four American-trained prisoners Toptani and Daci were given life imprisonment, Hoxha and Shehu twenty years each.

The rest received shorter sentences. However, none of them has reappeared since the trial. It is assumed by their friends and relations that they all perished at the hands of the Albanian secret police.

Although the Albanian authorities did all they could to publicise the trial, it received hardly a mention in the Western media. The alleged facts were so bizarre, the confessions so pathetic, the language of the prosecution so violent and extravagant that it all seemed like the usual Soviet lies, yet another Stalinist charade, and non-Albanian newspapers were disinclined even to refer to it. The Soviet press played it down too,[59] presumably because the Western allies' new aggressive policy against their empire's weakest member was something that they did not want to advertise. And so the event took place amid a glare of local Albanian publicity, but without the American or British public even knowing that these extraordinary acts had been carried out in their name.

On October 15th, undeterred by the fact that their four earlier protégés were still on trial for their lives, American intelligence dropped five more men near Blata mountain in the Dibra region: Hysen Salku, Hysen Bajrami, Ramazan Dalipi, Hajrulla Terpeza and Hakik Abdullah. Group leader Salku landed badly and broke both legs. (He had received no parachute training.) The other four tried to collect their equipment, but much of it was hanging by parachute lines from trees and had to be abandoned. They carried Salku 200 yards to a hiding place in the woods.

They tried to get some rest, but a few hours later dawn broke and they were attacked. Dalipi says, 'It was quite a big enemy force. There were machine-guns and mortars. They must have been waiting for us. They were in action against us so quickly.' Salku and Bajrami were killed. A bullet passed through Dalipi's clothing. He, Terpeza and Abdullah managed to escape, but they were completely lost. Salku was the only one who knew the Dibra area. The others were Albanians from Yugoslavia. They had no equipment either. So there was nothing for them to do except retreat. They made straight for the border and a week later reached Krčova, Dalipi's home town in Macedonia, where they begged some food and turned south towards Greece, crossing into friendly territory on October 31st. Their time in the field, four days in Albania and eleven in Yugoslavia, had been spent entirely on the run evading communist patrols.

The operation was therefore well and truly blown. Four of the American-trained infiltrators had been captured alive, two in November 1950 and two in July 1951. They had been interrogated, tried and sentenced after telling the Albanian police everything they knew. The names of almost all the trainees at the 'secret' school were mentioned during the trial, including some who had already escaped into Yugoslavia and others still being trained. Much of the story emerges from the trial evidence as published by the Albanian foreign ministry and one assumes that the communists had other sources of information too, that they knew more than they were prepared to publish.

Philby, their main source, was no longer working at the operation's heart, but he was still in touch with it indirectly through his SIS friends who sympathised with him and believed that he had been badly treated. He came to London from his Hertfordshire home several times every week and was often to be seen in London clubs with former colleagues, drinking deeply and complaining loudly. He was probably able to use these encounters to gather scraps of information about the secret operations he had previously controlled. And, of course, he was all the time in contact with his real employers, the Soviet secret service.

The information that they gathered during 1951 made it easier still for the Albanian and Soviet police to penetrate the exile centres. By the end of the year they knew every Albanian closely involved. All these men had families back home. They could be bribed and blackmailed into revealing vital facts.

For the Soviet police and their Albanian colleagues it was not a very challenging task. Philby had given them the breakthrough and plenty of time to thwart the invaders. They had merely to build up their sources, analyse the information, maintain normal vigilance, act on specific tip-offs and have their men strategically placed ready to pick the agents up as soon as they dropped from the sky.

9 The last great chance

Radio Tirana's powerful transmitters broadcast the October 1951 trial almost word for word. The Albanian trainees in Malta, Munich and Heidelberg heard it all loud and clear. They heard the broken voices of their tortured friends, men who a few months earlier had been living with them in Germany preparing Albania's liberation. Now they were in Enver Hoxha's hands broadcasting in great detail what he wanted them to say and what the Americans were doing.

Letters of complaint from the few survivors of the November 1950 mission began arriving at Company 4000 in Munich. Written in Yugoslavia and sent to Germany through the ordinary mail, they complained that nothing was being done to extricate them from the hands of the Yugoslav police or to help their families. One such letter, written by Rexh Berisha to Muhamet Hoxha, was even mentioned during the latter's trial as evidence of American-Yugoslav cooperation in the plot. Laci wrote to Rome, 'I urge you to help our members in Yugoslavia as soon as possible.'

It also became known around this time that doors were being opened for the emigration of east Europeans to Canada, Australia and the United States. The Albanian trainees realised that they were no longer limited to a choice between working for British or American intelligence and vegetating in a refugee camp. Other opportunities were available.

The result was a sudden and very serious decline in

morale among the trainees. Xhemal Laci wrote to monarchist headquarters in Rome, 'Some men have found out that the missions are going badly, that men have been killed and their families in Albania executed as well. Some also feel that they are making great sacrifices while the committee shows no interest in them or their families.'

The relationship between Legaliteti and Balli Kombëtar changed from one of rivalry to one of suspicion and bitter quarrel. The royalists fell out with their American captain, Thomas Mangelly, and accused him of anti-Zog bias. The explosion came over a ridiculous incident that winter. A platoon of royalists, after relieving a platoon of republicans on guard-duty, discovered that the latter had built an elaborate snow-structure in the shape of a Moslem tomb inscribed with King Zog's name.

Bame Morava, who had joined the company in June 1951 with eighty other Albanians from Greece, says, 'In those days I was such a royalist. If I'd found the man who did that I'd have killed him on the spot.' Laci also advised Rome that the culprit ought to be shot. The two factions were lined up opposite one another ready to open fire and civil war would have begun if Major Çaush Basho had not promised to find the guilty men. After frantic telegrams from Mangelly to Rome three Albanian leaders rushed up to Munich on the first train and with some difficulty calmed them down.

In the face of these problems several leading American and British officers involved in the affair were summoned in late October 1951 to a meeting in Rome to discuss past mistakes and future possibilities. Northrop recalls that the meeting began well with a dinner hosted by Joe Leib on Britain's election night, October 25th. After dinner they listened to the BBC overseas radio. Soon they were in a position to celebrate Labour's defeat and Winston Churchill's return to power. American guests observed that it augured well for the American election a year later when several men closely linked with the Committee for Free

Europe, including Dwight D. Eisenhower and the Dulles brothers, would be in line for high office.

Leib was determined to celebrate the Conservative victory by 'treating' his English visitors. He drove Harold Perkins and Anthony Northrop to a nightclub. It had just closed, but he persuaded the owner to reopen it. Wine began to flow, music was played and quantities of American taxpayers' money were spent. The evening's climax, Northrop remembers, was a parade of 'rather exotic-looking young women' in whose direction Leib gestured expansively with the words, 'Choose any one you like, Tony, and she's yours till breakfast-time.'

During the next days' discussions it was noted that the British operations fared better than the American ones and the policy of delivering agents by parachute was brought into question. The American side pointed out that unmarked aircraft provided the only means of delivering men quickly and accurately to the target area. They could only operate effectively in their home villages. Other parts of Albania were a closed book to them. If they were to be landed by sea or put across the Greek frontier, as the British had done, an elaborate system of guides would have to be provided. Albanian agents could be expected to find their way from the sea or the frontier to Korçë or Gjirokaster, but not to central or northern Albania, which was the sphere of American operation.

The British side were nevertheless worried by the American policy of dropping untrained men of mediocre physical capacity with heavy equipment at heights as low as 500 feet. It was then the minimum height for a highly trained parachutist, allowing 200 feet for the 'chute to develop, with very little left for the fall. For untrained men such a method was 'suicidal' according to Northrop: 'At that height they were very close to having their 'chutes open after they hit the ground, so to speak.' A few days earlier Hysen Salku had been killed in Albania after landing badly and breaking both legs.

A pilot flying at treetop level would have to 'rev' his engines very high, so as to be ready for a sudden push upwards. Once the fuselage door is opened, the air rushes in and the noise is deafening. Northrop says:

> It is no easy matter to fly an aircraft at fifty feet for half an hour, with hardly anything to navigate by, and then suddenly pull up to 500 feet and find the precise moment in your arc of ascent to put your men out of the door. Then it would have been quite terrifying for the Albanians who were not accustomed to parachuting. It's no reflection on their bravery. It used to frighten the life out of me and I was properly trained. If they'd never done it before, they'd have been thinking all kinds of things, but not what they needed to think about in order to survive.

In February 1952 Northrop began training groups of four or five Albanians near Chagford on the Devon moors. He soon found that most of them were men who, if they had appeared before a British army selection board, would not have been chosen for commando training. He says, 'Some of them, after I'd marched them twenty-five miles across Devon, weren't even fit to go to bed, let alone into action. They just weren't up to it physically.' He remembers asking his Broadway superiors, 'Have you ever marched twenty-five miles in a snowstorm? And in enemy-occupied country?' It is one thing, he pointed out, to walk twenty-five miles in fine weather over land where there is no reason for fear and quite another to do what his trainees were going to be expected to do. If they couldn't do it on the Devon moors, they certainly weren't going to be able to do it in Albania.

Northrop's reservations and a certain appreciation of the previous year's failures led to the British decision at this point to end their side of the operation. Fort Bin Jema continued briefly with a skeleton group of trainees under Anthony Newman's command. The facility was then dismantled under the direction of SIS deputy director

George Young and the trainees scattered throughout the world.

CIA, however, was undeterred. Stalin's excesses had in no way diminished and the Republican party hoped to achieve the presidency on a platform that included eastern Europe's liberation. Furthermore, in spite of its notable setbacks, the Albanian operation at last seemed to offer a chance to recoup past losses, justify earlier decisions and achieve success on a spectacular scale.

Most of the agents sent into Albania had fared badly. However, CIA had noted the brilliant success of one man, Hamit Matjani, a guerilla fighter who seemed able to enter Albania at will living off the land and retreating into Greece as soon as his job was done. He was a hero in the Robin Hood tradition, half brigand and half freedom-fighter, semi-literate but more cunning than any of the authorities – Italian, German or Albanian communist – who had tried to catch him. He first crossed into Greece in November 1947, following which he made twelve successful forays, always travelling on foot with two or three companions.

In summer 1951 King Zog visited the United States, ostensibly to buy property. On August 8th he and his nephew Prince Tati were received at the State Department by James C. Bornbright, deputy assistant secretary for European affairs,[60] for a ceremonial visit. However, the real reason for his visit was to discuss with Gratian Yatsevich and other OPC/CIA officers in Washington why the missions mounted from Germany had failed and how they might establish a more effective tactic. They agreed that Matjani was the man of the moment, the one fighter who had proved his ability to operate inside Albania and dodge communist patrols. He had helped the Americans to make rough maps showing police and army strongpoints. He gave them lists of sympathetic villages and potential allies, some of them officers in the Albanian army.

Yatsevich explained to the King that these officers wanted tangible proof of royal approval and commitment.

They also wanted proof of American backing. They would then move against communist power. A difficult question then arose. Which men were best qualified to enter Albania, with Matjani as their guide, and to provide the officers with the guarantees they wanted? The King replied that there was only one group with the necessary courage and authority, the men who had stayed with him throughout his exile and lived with him in Egypt now, his own Royal Guard.

Yatsevich selected eight Albanians of above-average intelligence for special training in radio and cipher work, not at the 'schloss' but at another secret school in the Frankfurt area. They spent most of 1952 learning map reading and intelligence evaluation as well as radio operation and maintenance, being trained (they were told) for a mission even more important and secret than anything that had gone before.

Every month the eight men were allowed a night out in a nearby city. Bame Morava, who was one of the eight, has vivid memories of this bizarre ritual: 'They used to dress us in American uniforms and take us there in two big cars after dark, so that we wouldn't remember the way. We had no documents, just a telephone number in case of emergency. They dropped us off in the main square, gave us some money, quite a lot of money, and told us to get drunk and find a woman.' Morava recalls that he and his friends refused the favours of local ladies. They were all married and they imagined at the time that it would only be a few months before they had beaten the communists and were back with their own families.

After a few months Morava and his friends were transferred to the new CIA base in Greece, established the previous year in the Kalanissia island group in the Halcyon sea a few miles north of Corinth. As part of Britain's policy of 'handing on the torch' in the Balkans, CIA had been encouraged to take over nearly all the British secret networks and installations. The United States was bearing the burden of the anti-Soviet resistance movements on the basis of British experience and the decision to transfer the island to American control was taken by Greece's military ruler Alexander Papagos in recognition of the need to help the United States to win the Cold War by destabilising the Soviet Union's satellites.

The Kalanissia or 'beautiful islands', so called because they provide water and safe haven, lie three miles north of Strava, a settlement on the Greek mainland fifteen miles north of Loutraki, Posidhonia and the western mouth of the Corinth canal. The largest of the three, known as Panaghia, was disguised as a radar station complete with dummy revolving aerials and designated as a military zone by Greece to make sure local fishermen kept their distance from it. In fact, it accommodated teams of refugees from Albania, Bulgaria and the Soviet Union who, under American supervision, maintained radio contact with OPC/CIA agents in the field. It was also the control point for clandestine radio broadcasts and other propaganda efforts against the Hoxha regime.

Dino Mavros had left Barclay's and Leatham's service and was now under contract to CIA to make a weekly two-hour voyage to the island from Posidhonia with supplies of bread, vegetables and fruit. The only other Greek visitor was a monk who came occasionally to tend crops growing in the garden of a deserted monastery. When Mavros was up the Adriatic 'on business' or when the weather was bad a light aircraft from Athens dropped supplies on to the island by parachute.

High-speed boats based in Kalanissia went up the Albanian coastline on various errands. Gaqi Gogo remembers hearing that on one occasion several dozen buoys carrying Albanian National Committee flags were let go near Corfu and allowed to drift on to the mainland shore. Usually, though, boats left Kalanissia on radio work. Morava went on several voyages up as far as the Yugoslav border monitoring Albanian-language broadcasts and reporting on their audibility. He also sent Morse messages from the boat to real or imaginary agents. The security police, it was hoped, would think they were being transmitted from inside Albania.

King Zog returned from the United States in October 1951. He had bought a substantial property and allegedly paid for it with a bucket of jewellery. Then during the 1951–2 winter Yatsevich joined him in Egypt and they discussed with Hysen Selmani, colonel of the Royal Guard, which men were to join Matjani for the crucial mission. The three finally chosen were Zenel Shehu, Halil Branica and Haxhi Gjyle. In early 1952 Matjani wrote several letters to royalist headquarters in Rome. Based on his many incursions into Albania in 1951–2, they confirmed American intelligence's impression that the moment was ripe for a substantial effort.

Matjani wrote in a private letter on March 6th:

> The economic situation in the country is very bad. So is the military situation. The conscript army lacks all motivation. They have no choice but to serve and they just wait for the day when something will happen. There are officers with doubts about the regime also. The only ones truly motivated are the Sigurimi [secret police]. The ordinary police are half and half. New units have been created with the sole purpose of fighting the groups entering the country. These men are kept isolated from the rest of the armed forces and they live very well, better than officers.

The lines, written by a man who had been in and out of Albania frequently, fitted in well with the CIA theory that their operations had in spite of everything made an impact on the Hoxha regime and that it would take no more than one 'big push' to topple the communists. The contacts that Matjani had made with Albanian army officers were to be the key to this effort.

The three men chosen from the Royal Guard prepared

for their departure and the King gave each of them a bag of gold. Zenel Shehu said goodbye to Queen Geraldine alone. He had guarded her since the family's flight from the Italian army in April 1939 and their parting was an emotional one. Shehu gave her the gold and a box of personal belongings, asking her to keep them for him or, if he did not return, for his family. In early March they left Alexandria by ship for Marseilles with Hysen Selmani and Princesses Maxhide and Ruhije. Since it was necessary to explain away their sudden departure, Zog told friends in Egypt that they had gone to France to guard or look after the princesses. They would then be going to the United States to manage his new property.

On March 9th the four men reached Paris and checked in to the Hotel Lutetia at 43 Boulevard Raspail. Two days later an American giving his name as 'Field' came to the hotel to discuss with Selmani the mechanics of a swift and discreet transfer to Athens. On March 14th OPC men arrived with two cars and they set off for the German border. Shortly before the frontier the cars stopped and the Albanians slipped into a wood to change into American uniform. As American soldiers travelling in American military vehicles they could cross the border without being checked by French or German police. They drove to a safe house near Munich, spent a week there eating and resting, then were flown to Athens. They passed through the airport without formality and reached another safe house in Piraeus on March 26th.[61]

Shehu, Branica and Gjyle spent the next month being trained by American officers at Hadjinikillis in the Athens area. They learnt mainly map reading and weapon handling. They were introduced to Matjani and to the two other men who would be accompanying them, Xhelo Tresova and Tahir Prenci. Prenci was to be the group's radio operator. At the end of the training period an American known to them as Colonel John took Shehu and Selmani on one side: 'He told us that we were going on a very important mission, that we should be careful because the Sigurimi were strong, that our aim must be to build friendly bases and gather information. Every base must be kept very secret, he said. He showed each one to me on the maps without marking them in any way in case they fell into the hands of Sigurimi. The bases were in Martanesh, Bulqizë and Mati.'

On April 27th they were flown from Athens to Kastoria, a point near the Albanian border only fifteen miles from Korçë. The next day Greek officers escorted them as far as the frontier and covered them as they crossed. As they approached Gramshi, an Albanian border village, Branica became ill and walked back into Greece. The others, guided by Tresova who knew the area intimately, were taken to a friendly base near Korçë where they were given refreshment before pressing on northwards to Matjani's home area.

After they reached the Mati area safely Matjani, Gjyle and Tresova turned back towards Greece leaving Shehu and Prenci with anti-communist groups recruited by Matjani the previous year. Throughout the 1952 summer OPC representatives in Greece were pleased to find themselves at last in regular contact with agents in the field. Prenci, well trained in Morse and cipher, reported that they were making useful allies, that they even had three Sigurimi men willing to go to Greece for debriefing and training in resistance work. Halil Branica recovered from his illness and on August 4th the Polish airmen parachuted him into Albania at a time and place suggested in one of Prenci's messages.

Quantities of equipment were also dropped at Prenci's request: gold sovereigns, machine-guns, ammunition, radios, binoculars, woollen underwear, hats, trousers and a can of beige paint. American intelligence was greatly encouraged. It indicated that opposition bases were being established and equipped in an orderly fashion. There was only one matter that gave cause for concern. In one of his early messages Prenci explained that he had broken his right arm and was therefore transmitting his Morse with the left hand.

In Company 4000 morale continued to decline and Xhemal Laci wrote to Rome, 'We are losing face with our American friends because of our failure to fulfil what is required of us and also because our people are generally not up to their expectations . . . There is a marked difference since last year.' Later on he reported an increase in the number of men leaving the company for Canada and he asked Rome to prevent the issue of so many invitations. However, as if to compensate for this gloomy news, coming as it did on top of the 1951 disasters, optimistic reports from Shehu's, Branica's and Prenci's bases in central Albania continued to reach American intelligence headquarters in Athens.

CIA suffered a serious setback at the end of 1952 when it emerged that their entire covert operation in Poland, the 'WiN' organisation, had from the outset been controlled by the Soviet police and Polish colleagues. Leaders of the plot were arrested and put on trial. Documents were reproduced in the Polish press and many articles were printed about the 'treason' of Polish émigrés. At the same time, in spite of this success on the part of their security services, the Soviet bloc seemed gripped by panic and hysteria. On December 3rd former Czechoslovak party secretary Rudolf Slansky and ten other former leaders were hanged in Prague after a ludicrous show trial. On January 10th, 1953, the Soviet press announced the discovery of a 'doctors' plot' to poison Stalin and his friends. It was a few days after Eisenhower had become US president with John Foster Dulles as his secretary of state and Allen Dulles as CIA director.

It was therefore a good moment for CIA to step up the Albanian enterprise. The messages from Shehu and Branica were becoming more and more triumphant. Their position as King Zog's loyal lieutenants had, it seemed, tipped the scale. Their network of bases was expanding. There was now a nucleus of army and police officers ready to move against the communist regime. The parachuted equipment had been distributed and would soon be put to use. What they needed now, they said, was for Hamit Matjani to join them with suitable guides ready to escort some of their new recruits into Greece to help with final preparations and give American intelligence an insider's view of Albania's defences. They added that in the interest of speed and security it would be better for Matjani's team not to march their way through southern Albania as they had on every previous occasion. Their bases were secure enough now for Matjani to come in by parachute.

Yatsevich flew to Alexandria to discuss the proposal with King Zog. Both CIA and the King were excited about the possibilities. At last there seemed a real chance that they would achieve their objective and remove Albania from Soviet control. Only one dark shadow hung over the plan. Prenci had still not reverted to his natural 'fist'. Every Morse operator had his own individual way of tapping the key and headquarters were sure that it was not being tapped in Prenci's normal style.

Normally this would arouse deep concern. The King and his American sponsors could in no way put Matjani, their trump card, into play on the basis of messages of doubtful origin. On the other hand, Prenci had explained why his 'fist' was different and on being tested with prearranged signals he had on every occasion sent the correct coded reply. It was worrying, but the Americans felt inclined to continue the mission. The stakes were very high, they explained. They had done all they could to investigate the discrepancy and it would be wrong now to abort a mission of such importance on the basis of unproven suspicion.

Queen Geraldine suggested a way of solving the dilemma:

> I remembered that Zenel Shehu had given me his personal valuables to look after. No one else knew about this. So I said to the Americans, 'Ask Zenel where he left his personal belongings.' If everything was all right he would reply 'with the lady of the house' or 'with mother' or some such expression. So the Americans did this and

> they got an answer back from the agents in Albania to leave them in peace and stop asking stupid questions. And the Americans accepted it. They didn't take me seriously. They preferred to rely on the code phrases, but there were several people who knew about these phrases. The communists only had to torture one of them or have a spy in their midst and they could find out about the phrases. The information about Zenel's things was known only to me personally.

Hamit Matjani was therefore kitted out and invited to prepare himself for the journey. Stalin's death on March 5th, 1953, seemed to make the moment even more propitious and they agreed that the drop would take place on May Day, when the Sigurimi were busy celebrating. Matjani, Naum Sula and Gani Malushi were duly parachuted on to a prearranged spot in the Mati area. Reassuring messages from the field continued to reach CIA headquarters in Athens. However, months passed and none of the carefully arranged plans showed any sign of materialising. As 1953 drew to a close the coded messages' ring of authenticity was beginning to sound hollow. The blow fell on New Year's Eve when Albanian radio announced that all the men so carefully trained for this most vital part of the operation – Matjani, Shehu, Branica, Sula, Malushi and several locally recruited friends – were in the hands of the Sigurimi awaiting trial.

The facts that emerged during the great show trial of April 1954 in Tirana revealed a catastrophe far beyond American intelligence's worst nightmares. It transpired that Shehu had been captured almost as soon as he arrived in the Mati two years earlier. His radio operator Tahir Prenci had disappeared, either killed in action or, as many Albanians believe, enlisted in support of the communist cause. For eighteen months the Sigurimi, advised by their Soviet colleagues, had concocted and transmitted the radio messages on which American decisions were based. They had cleaned up the whole network and Hamit Matjani, the man who had eluded them so often, had been dropped into their hands from an American aircraft.

For an entire week the Albanian exile communities in Rome, Athens, Munich and Alexandria listened in horror as Radio Tirana presented the world with a chronicle of their political and military activities. The Sigurimi had done their work well. By interrogating their American-trained prisoners, using Soviet methods, they had discovered all the essential facts not only about the Shehu/Matjani operation, but also about the five years of intrigue that formed the background. Several prominent Americans and all the main Albanian exile leaders were mentioned during the proceedings. The trial's legal form was grotesque, but its basic facts are confirmed by Albanian survivors and they are in the author's view accurate.

On April 12th King Zog and his family sat round the radio in their Alexandria villa as the judge in Tirana found the accused guilty and pronounced sentence. Shehu, Branica, Sula and Malushi were to be shot, Matjani to be hanged, in the judge's gruesome phrase, 'to suffer death by the cord'. Young Prince Leka, who had just celebrated his fifteenth birthday, was deeply moved. Shehu and Branica, the doomed officers of the Royal Guard, were like uncles to him, men he had grown up with and come to love. His reaction to the judge's words was along the lines of Albanian tradition. He swore a blood feud against Enver Hoxha and his family. The feud became his life's work and thirty years later he still pursues it.

10 The ruin of their hopes

A reign of terror was launched throughout Albania. Ermenji says, 'The communists executed not only the Albanians who had been parachuted into the country, but also all those with whom they had made contact, about 400 people in the Mati area alone.' This was not all. When a man was executed, his family was arrested and detained for an indefinite period, the women for work in the fields, the men in the mines. Conditions were bad and many died. The number of people who suffered this fate as a result of the entire debacle is not known, though it is certainly several thousand, a significant part of Albania's population, then less than two million.

It was, of course, the end of the Albanian operation. Relations between the Albanian exile groups and the sponsors had been deteriorating for two years. In 1952 Abas Ermenji asked his Balli Kombëtar followers to stop going on missions. After this, even though Hasan Dosti remained as committee chairman, the operation went on with no real republican representation. Members of the 'Independenza' group, some of whom had worked with the Italians during the war, were moved in to take their place.

Vasil Andoni says, 'We broke away because the Americans gave us to understand that we must work under their orders, since they were the paymasters. We told them that we would prefer to fight on our own, without American money, if necessary in the refugee camps.' There were tensions in Rome too between Leib and Archie Lyall, the British representative, made worse by Maclean's and Burgess's disappearance and the Philby row. Andoni remembers being continually asked by Leib how often he had met Lyall and what they had discussed.

On June 22nd, 1954, Captain Frederic W. Pechin wrote to Xhemal Laci from headquarters of the 37th Labor Supervision Company of the American army in Germany dismissing him from Company 4000. Laci had, according to Pechin, caused trouble among Albanians in the American service. 'You repeatedly played cards in the canteen with enlisted members of the company,' he wrote. Company 4000 was no longer a disciplined unit. They felt grief at the loss of friends and family. Although they did not yet know about Philby, they knew that there must be traitors monitoring their activities. They felt betrayed by their sponsors and they no longer wished to continue the fight. The company was disbanded while on the point of falling apart. The Heidelberg 'schloss' and the CIA-controlled Greek island were closed down. The surviving Albanians were resettled, most of them in the United States but others in Canada, Australia, Britain, France, Belgium and Germany.

They were betrayed, they say, not only by Kim Philby, whom many of them hold personally responsible for the death of friends and relatives, not only by fellow Albanians who talked carelessly or, as they assume happened in a few cases, were bribed or blackmailed into giving information to the communist side, but also by their American and British sponsors. Abas Ermenji speaks with particular bitterness: 'Our "allies" wanted to make use of Albania as a guinea-pig, without caring about the human losses, for an absurd enterprise that was condemned to failure. This failure was roughly the same as that suffered by the Cuban exiles in the Bay of Pigs episode a few years later.'

Ermenji and others complain that their innocence and trust were exploited by the secret services of two powerful and sophisticated countries. They were recruited, they say, on the understanding that the United States and Britain wanted to liberate Albania from communism. And on this basis they were happy to agree. They would fight and they would sacrifice lives, not only their own, but also those of their brothers, wives and children.

They were ready to fight for Albania but for no other cause. And this is why, they say, the truth was kept from them. They were not told of the many other reasons why the operation was taking place, about the need to relieve communist pressure on Greece in the civil war, about the decision to retaliate against Stalin's aggressive moves, to punish Enver Hoxha for his treatment of British agents in 1944–5 and for the Corfu channel incident. They were not advised that the conspiracy against communist Albania was no more than a single move in a great game of geopolitical chess and that they, the 'little men', were the pawns most likely to be taken.

American and British intelligence men who took part in the conspiracy point out in reply that it seemed obviously right at the time to make use of their Second World War experience of secret operations. Similar plots against Nazi Germany had been mounted only five years earlier and many had been successful. It would have been over-squeamish, indeed a dereliction of duty, to remain passive in the face of Stalin's challenge. The West, to its shame, had abandoned Poland and Czechoslovakia to Stalin's tender mercies. They had to do something to wipe out this stain.

True, they say, the operation failed. But they could not anticipate that police control over the local people would be so tight and effective under communism, far more so than under Nazi occupation. Nor could they have foreseen Philby's treachery. Anyway, they say, even though the liberation of Albania was not achieved, the United States and Britain did succeed in giving Stalin an effective demonstration of the West's will to retaliate, thereby saving other countries. If the West had faltered, Stalin would have resurrected the Greek civil war, snuffed out Tito's rebellion and boosted the Italian communists. Democracy in western Europe would not have survived this onslaught.

They concede that the Albanian exiles were not told the full truth. But, they say, Western intelligence services cannot always observe the rules of fair play when fighting the Soviet adversary. The Albanian exiles who fought under their auspices were all enthusiastic volunteers, men who from the outset begged to be given the dignity of fighting men rather than being left to rot in refugee camps. They knew the risks they were running.

Most of those who went into the field, it is appreciated, did not escape. However, casualties were always envisaged, by the agents as well as by the sponsors. American and British agents would have shared these dangers, as they had in wartime, if there had not been compelling political reasons against this.

They accept that they committed a violation of international law. However, they say, Hoxha had no right to claim the protection of any such law. He had usurped power in Albania by force and failed to hold democratic elections. He had defied the International Court over the Corfu incident and allowed his territory to be used to attack Greek government forces. He had only himself to blame if he was treated in similar fashion.

The stakes were very high, they say. The Cold War was at its worst and real war between the Soviet Union and the West was considered likely. In battle it is sometimes necessary to give up a platoon so as to facilitate a battalion's withdrawal. If 'pawns' have to be 'sacrificed' in order to deter an adversary from aggression, then so be it, it must be done. And in extreme cases, when vital interests are truly at risk, the victims must be deceived.

It was therefore an honourable enterprise, at least at the outset, and if it had succeeded it would certainly have given Albania a form of democracy. Still, its execution was marred by massive flaws. CIA/OPC and SIS were misled in the first place by over-optimistic intelligence from Albania and by the enthusiasm of Albanian émigrés. Also they underestimated the Soviet Union's success in perfecting systems of internal control in their satellite countries. They did not appreciate how easy it would be for the communist police, controlling Albania as they did, to gather intelligence about the operation and penetrate its west European centres.

They chose men of limited physical strength to do jobs better suited to trained commandos. They sent radio operators into the field without proper instruction in cipher or Morse. They gave the men no practice parachute jumps and in most cases only two or three weeks' instruction in guerilla warfare. Often they landed the men in the wrong place and no group ever got the heavy equipment that should have been dropped with them.

One question is especially hard to answer. Why did CIA/ OPC continue dropping men into Albania, sacrificing lives by the hundred, when it was quite obvious that the operation was having no result? It was clear surely that, while the 1949 sea landings achieved mediocre success, the airborne landings in 1951 ended disastrously. Kim Philby, the operation's former joint commander, was suspected of being a traitor. Was it not obvious at that point that the whole operation was thoroughly betrayed? Was it not clear that Hoxha's police had pulled such a tight noose that guerilla groups could no longer operate? At that point, surely, they should have stopped sending the men in?

The bizarre decisions of the operation's later stages can only be explained by recalling the atmosphere of the time in the run up to the November 1952 American elections. The liberation of Soviet satellites was a popular political platform. CIA was building up a propaganda and espionage effort all over eastern Europe. There was, however, only one 'sharp' operation, Albania, where American protégés were actually in armed conflict with the other side. It had taken years to obtain political clearance for the scheme and to build up its bureaucratic momentum. It seemed to have failed, but it was hard to take the decision to end it, thereby admitting that so much time, money and human life had been spent in vain.

British intelligence took no part in these final disasters and the agents they trained fared better than those sponsored by Americans in Germany. Still, it was one of their senior officers who betrayed the operation from the outset. American intelligence is quick to mention this aspect of British responsibility. It appears in the affidavit by Louis J. Dube quoted in the introduction to this book and in *The CIA's Secret Operations*, an account cleared by the author's former employers, in which Harry Rositzke writes, 'There is little question that Philby not only informed Moscow of overall British and American planning, but provided details on the individual dispatch of agent teams before they arrived in Albania. No one in London or Washington, of course, knew at the time why the disaster was so total.'[62]

However, Enver Hoxha is no longer the Soviet Union's friend, having quarrelled with Nikita Khrushchev in the early 1960s, and he prefers to give credit to his own Sigurimi rather than to a Soviet spy. He writes:

> We forced the captured agents to make radio contact with their espionage centres in Italy and elsewhere, hence to play our game . . . The bands of the criminals who were dropped in by parachute or infiltrated across the border at our request came like lambs to the slaughter, while the armaments and other materials which they dropped or brought with them went to our account. . . . Our famous radio game brought about the ignominious failure of the plans of the foreign enemy, not the merits of a certain Kim Philby, as some have claimed.[63]

To what extent, then, was Philby responsible for the failure? Clearly he was not the operation's only flaw. He did not, for instance, cause the debacle of the Shehu/Matjani mission mentioned by Hoxha in the lines above. This episode took place long after his recall to London in June 1951. After that date he received no first-hand information on the Albanian affair. He was in touch with Soviet spies in London. He could tell them the background, but nothing new.

Still, Philby was in the author's view one of the main causes of the disaster. He betrayed the plan for nearly two years. He alerted the Soviet Union about the first seaborne landings in October 1949. He gave them details too about the cross-frontier infiltrations of mid-1950 and the first American parachute drop in November 1950. These first operations did not succeed, but they were not disastrous. They would have been more successful if Philby had not betrayed them and perhaps provided a basis for real success. As it was, he gave the communists a crucial advantage. By the time he was recalled they had tightened their grip and found other agents to replace him.

Former OPC European director Frank Lindsay agrees with some of these criticisms. It was unethical as well as foolish, he says, to carry on sacrificing human lives in the operation's latter stages, especially since the West was not willing to give them appropriate training and back-up. Rositzke, also expressing a CIA view, also delivers a stark verdict: 'The Albanian operation was the first and only attempt by Washington to unseat a communist regime within the Soviet orbit by paramilitary means. It taught a clear lesson to the war planners. Even a weak regime could not be overthrown by covert paramilitary actions alone.'

It seems therefore that a lesson was learnt, at least as far as the Soviet Union's European orbit was concerned, though it did not cure the United States of the idea of using exiles to overthrow unfriendly governments, as was shown in Cuba in 1961.

It was the end of the Albanian operation and East-West relations began to improve. Stalin was dead, his police chief Lavrenti Beria was purged. Millions were being released from the labour camps as Khrushchev prepared to denounce Stalin's excesses. OPC had been set up in 1948 on an *ad hoc* basis, to remove central Europe from Soviet control. By 1954 it was clear to the West that this would not be achieved in the short term. CIA, now embracing OPC, was ordered to restrict its activities inside the Soviet bloc to espionage, propaganda and other less violent pursuits.

The Cold War was over. An uneasy sort of order and normality began to govern relations between the two superpowers. The Soviet Union scaled down the crudest of its subversive activities in Europe. In return the West seemed ready to accept Stalin's interpretation of the Yalta agreement, including the Soviet Union's right to a 'defensive' ring of buffer states, a new Russian empire. Kim Philby lived on in limbo until 1963 when he defected to Moscow, where he now lives as a colonel in the Soviet secret service.

Albania quarrelled with the Soviet Union and disappeared into obscurity, the 'purity' of its communism strengthened by the operation's legacy. Enver Hoxha, approaching his eightieth year, continues to rule his lonely country as the world's longest surviving dictator. He has banned private ownership of the most modest kind, he keeps large sections of his population in labour camps, he prevents all but the most casual contact with foreigners and he has abolished religion. Every now and again in a speech he mentions the American and British 'invasion' of 1949–53 and uses it to justify his policy of isolation.

The American and British intelligence men who tried to change Albania's government moved on to other things. Smiley went back to the army and commanded his regiment. Amery and McLean went into the House of Commons where they maintained their ideological fight against communism. Hare left MI6 in 1961, became head of a well-known British publishing house, then chairman of the London *Financial Times*. Yatsevich stayed on in CIA, becoming station chief in Teheran and close adviser to the Shah of Iran. Low became financial consultant to shipping millionaire Stavros Niarchos. Leib was made a public relations officer in the Pepsi-Cola company. Burke achieved national fame as chairman of the New York Yankees baseball club.

The Albanians fared less interestingly. A few prospered to the extent of having jobs, wives and children. Bardhyl Gerveshi works as an engineer near London and Bame Morava owns a restaurant in Canada, named after the baby daughter he left behind in Albania in 1951. Most of them, however, languish in the small world of an exile community with no work and little knowledge of language. In the United States there are communities several thousand strong, for instance in the New York area, where they thrive on émigré politics. In London or Paris though there are only a few dozen fellow countrymen. Life is poor and lonely.

Their consolation is the fact that they were the only émigré community who actually took up arms and fought against one of the governments of Stalin's empire. And, in spite of all the failure and suffering, they are very glad to have done so and would willingly repeat the attempt, so deep is their commitment to an Albania free of communism. Meanwhile they have time on their hands to recreate memories of comrades-in-arms who perished, of wives and brothers who were killed in reprisal. Even so, they insist, the attempt was worthwhile.

Bitterness creeps into their voices only when they recall that the big nations who sponsored them so enthusiastically in 1949 have either forgotten about them or want them to be forgotten, that thirty-five years later they still do everything they can to prevent it being known that the brief alliance ever existed.

Notes and References

INTRODUCTION

1. Name changed at his own request
2. *My Silent War*, Kim Philby, p. 110

CHAPTER ONE

3. *The Anglo-American Threat to Albania*, Enver Hoxha, p. 42
4. Foreign Office 371/43549
5. War Office 204/9535
6. FO 371/58474
7. *Sons of the Eagle*, Julian Amery, p. 309
8. ibid. p. 314
9. ibid. p. 315

CHAPTER TWO

10. Documents on American Foreign Relations, p. 635
11. FO 371/78434
12. FO 371/72108
13. State Department 711. 75/1-1 448
14. FO 371/78230
15. SD 875.00/7-2848
16. SD 875.00/5-748
17. FO 371/72117
18. *Time and Tide* (London), January 22nd, 1949
19. The *Observer* (London), January 29th, 1978
20. Statements to Committee 3 of the UN General Assembly, October 4th and October 15th, 1948

21. FO 371/71687
22. ibid.
23. FO 371/71687
24. FO 371/77623
25. *Strategic Intelligence Digest – Albania*. Issued by United States Army, May 1948
26. *My Silent War*, p. 117

CHAPTER THREE

27. SD 875.00/12-948
28. *Sons of the Eagle*, p. 286

CHAPTER FIVE

29. *My Silent War*, p. 111
30. ibid. p. 115
31. National Security Council document 10/2
32. *New York Times*, March 27th, 1950
33. SD 840.00/6-2149
34. SD 875.00/9-1949

CHAPTER SIX

35. National Security Council/58 – September 14th, 1949
36. Joint Chiefs of Staff 1654/4 – October 21st, 1949
37. SD 875.00/9-1449
38. FO 371/78443
39. FO 371/78213
40. SD 875.00/8-2649
41. *Foreign Relations of the US 1949*, Vol VI, p. 386
42. FO 371/78444
43. SD 860H.00/9-2149
44. FO 371/78223
45. FO 371/78211
46. *New York Times*, November 4th, 1949
47. *Ethnikos Agon* (Yanina) March 29th, 1950
48. Name changed at his own request
49. NSC 58/2

CHAPTER SEVEN

50. Xhemal Laci's and Gaqi Gogo's quotes are from archive of the Legaliteti Movement made available to the author privately
51. *My Silent War*, p. 119

CHAPTER EIGHT

52. Name changed at his own request
53. *No Colours or Crest*, Peter Kemp, p. 273
54. *Procès Contre Les Espions et Agents de Diversion du Service des États Imperialistes Envoyés en Albanie*, p. 59
55. *Procès Contre Les Espions . . .*, p. 34
56. *Philby, The Spy Who Betrayed a Generation*, Bruce Page, David Leitch, Phillip Knightley, p. 211
57. *Procès Contre Les Espions . . .*, p. 49
58. ibid. p. 19
59. See *Krasny Flot* (Moscow), October 9th and October 12th, 1951. *Pravda*, October 27th, 1951

CHAPTER NINE

60. SD 767.11/8-851
61. Transcript of the April 1954 Tirana trial, made available to the author privately

CHAPTER TEN

62. *The CIA's Secret Operations*, Harry Rositzke, p. 171
63. *The Anglo-American Threat to Albania*, Enver Hoxha, p. 426

Select Bibliography

Julian Amery, *Sons of the Eagle: A Study in Guerilla War*, London, Macmillan, 1948

Michael Burke, *Outrageous Good Fortune*, Boston, Little Brown, 1984.

Blanche Wiesen Cook, *The Declassified Eisenhower: A Divided Legacy*, New York, Doubleday, 1981

William R. Corson, *The Armies of Ignorance: The Rise of the American Intelligence Empire*, New York, Dial Press/James Wade, 1967

Raymond Dennett and Robert K. Turner (editors), *Documents of American Foreign Relations, Vol X, Jan 1–Dec 31, 1948*, World Peace Foundation/Princeton University Press, 1950

Foreign Relations of the United States, 1949, Vols V and VI, Washington, United States Government Printing Office, 1977

Harry Hamm, *Albania: China's Beachhead in Europe*, New York, Frederick A. Praeger, 1963

Enver Hoxha, *The Anglo-American Threat to Albania: Memoirs of the National Liberation War*, Tirana, '8 Nentori', 1982

Quentin Hughes, *Britain in the Mediterranean and the Defence of her Naval Stations*, Liverpool, Penpaled Books, 1981

Peter Kemp, *No Colours or Crest*, London, Cassell, 1958

Stanislaw Kluz, *W Potrzasku Dziejowym, WiN na szlaku AK, Rozwiązania i Dokumentacja*, London, Katolicki Ośrodek Wydawniczy 'Veritas', 1978

Anton Logoreci, *The Albanians: Europe's Forgotten Survivors*, London, Victor Gollancz, 1977

Victor Marchetti and John D. Marks, *The CIA and the Cult of Intelligence*, New York, Alfred A. Knopf, 1974

Bruce Page, David Leitch, Phillip Knightley, *Philby, The Spy Who Betrayed a Generation*, London, André Deutsch, 1968

Kim Philby, *My Silent War*, London, Macgibbon & Kee, 1968

Thomas Powers, *The Man Who Kept Secrets: Richard Helms and the CIA*, New York, Alfred A. Knopf, 1979

Procès Contre Les Espions et Agents de Diversion du Service des États Imperialistes Envoyés en Albanie, Tirana, Ministry of Foreign Affairs, 1952

Arben Puto, *From the Annals of British Diplomacy (The Anti-Albanian plans of Great Britain during the Second World War according to Foreign Office documents of 1939–44)*, Tirana, '8 Nentori', 1981

David Smiley, *Albanian Assignment*, London, Chatto and Windus, 1984.

Anthony Verrier, *Through the Looking Glass: British Foreign Policy in an Age of Illusion*, London, Jonathan Cape, 1983

Nigel West, *A Matter of Trust, MI5 1945–72*, London, Weidenfeld & Nicolson, 1982

Nigel West, *MI6: British Secret Intelligence Service Operations, 1909–45*, London, Weidenfeld & Nicolson, 1983

Index

Index

Index